W9-ARP-042

Home Cooking

WITH AMY COLEMAN

✳

Produced by Marjorie Poore Productions

Photography by Darla Furlani

MPP BOOKS

✴ Acknowledgments

Numerous people made tremendous contributions to this book and the HOME COOKING television series. Like many television projects, this one would have never come to life had it not been for the visionary group at KitchenAid Portable Appliances who truly believe in the concept of home cooking and whose goal of helping home cooks is embedded in everything they do—whether it's making a better kitchen appliance or bringing cooking lessons, like the ones found in HOME COOKING, to millions of viewers around the country. I'd especially like to thank Tom Welke and Brian Maynard from KitchenAid who have guided this project with exceptional leadership and support.

We were also fortunate to have host/cooking teacher, Amy Coleman, join our team. She has an extraordinary talent in her ability to teach, her knowledge and skill, and her contagious enthusiasm for cooking.

Numerous other companies provided support for the project, such as Benziger Family Winery, Le Creuset, who provided us with many colorful cookware pieces from its outstanding line, the beautiful Metropolitan Hotel in downtown Vancouver for accommodating our guests in such wonderful surroundings,

President's Choice food products for an incredible assortment of high-quality food products to use in the making of the recipes, and Henckels for its superior cutlery. We were also fortunate to have the high-quality and versatile Calphalon cookware on our set, plus some beautiful aprons, chef's coats, chef's pants, and other wearable items from Chefwear. Also, thanks to Architectural/Plastics for its beautiful, durable, and versatile serving/preparation boards.

We also owe a debt of gratitude to PBS stations across the country who have given so much valuable airtime to cooking programs and to the viewers who tune in.

Lastly, I would like to thank my partner, Alec Fatalevich, who provided invaluable guidance, wisdom, and support through every phase of the project.

Marjorie Poore

I would like to thank my mother and father and my husband for all of their support.

Amy Coleman

Home Cooking with Amy Coleman © 1997 by Marjorie Poore Productions
Photography by Darla Furlani
Food stylist: Michel Poitras

Project management and editing: Meesha Halm
Design: Kari Perin, Perin + Perin
Production: Kristen Wurz

ISBN 09651095-1-8
Printed in Hong Kong

10 9 8 7 6 5 4 3 2

MPP Books
363 14th Avenue, San Francisco CA 94118

Permissions

Contents

Introduction

For some, cooking is an art form; for others, it's a hobby, and for yet others, it can be a mundane task or even a frightening challenge. No matter what someone's attitude about cooking is, there is usually at least one common thread that joins everyone— the appreciation of a delicious, home-cooked meal made with care and love.

This book brings together an incredible assortment of recipes that we believe will give home cooks many hours of inspiration in the kitchen. All the recipes are from the public television series, HOME COOKING with Amy Coleman. The programs included guest cookbook authors who added a wonderful dimension to the programs. In each case, we asked them to pick their most popular or favorite recipes and something that represents home cooking to them. In many cases a bit of nostalgia kicked in. Superstar chef Michael Chiarello from Napa Valley's culinary mecca, Tra Vigne, chose a pasta dish he makes at home nearly every Sunday morning with his three daughters. Best-selling cookbook author—and walking food and wine encyclopedia—Sharon Tyler Herbst, picked the cheesecake that always gets the most "ooh's and ah's" from her cooking students. Bon Appetit food editor and cookbook author, Kristine Kidd, who taste-tests hundreds of dishes a year, picked the "best shortbread" cookie recipe she ever tried. West Coast food writer, James McNair, who has written over thirty cookbooks, shared his all-time favorite pizzas from his best-selling

pizza cookbooks. The fun and talented Lora Brody, a friend to any beginner in the kitchen, chose a wonderful turkey breast recipe because it's "perfect for starter cooks," but in reality, it's perfect for any cook. Another talented cookbook author, Marlene Sorosky, came up with her top recommendations for a dinner party, including a spectacular eggplant torte. Even professional chefs, such as Culinary Olympics medal winner, Michael Noble, had their "home-cooked" favorites. His is a popular pancake served at the world-famous DIVA restaurant at the Metropolitan Hotel in Vancouver. (The recipe, he confesses, comes from his mom!) Martha Rose Shulman, another highly respected and popular food writer, picked a nachos recipe that she makes frequently for her own dinner parties. There was even a killer banana cake made by pastry chef, Wayne Brachman, who specializes in southwestern desserts. Another guest chef from Vancouver, Margaret Chisholm, picked some dishes indigenous to her beloved Northwest, including a special salmon dish cooked Native-American-style. For grilling, we got someone who knows his marinades—the exuberant and incredibly talented Canadian chef, Ted Reader. And finally, we were very fortunate to have a special holiday meal made from the outstanding Williams-Sonoma cookbook collection and prepared by the vivacious, multitalented Tori Ritchie.

Along with this, we have a wonderful group of recipes from our effervescent and talented host and cooking teacher, Amy Coleman, who presents the kinds of dishes that reflect what she believes home cooking is all about: delicious, approachable food, made with readily available ingredients, for which perfectionism is not required; food that one can say was "made from the heart."

So there you have it, an incredible assortment of recipes from an amazingly talented group of food experts and cooks who selected recipes for the kind of food they think of as "home cooking" and that they make in their homes. It just doesn't get any better or more delicious.

—Marjorie Poore, Producer

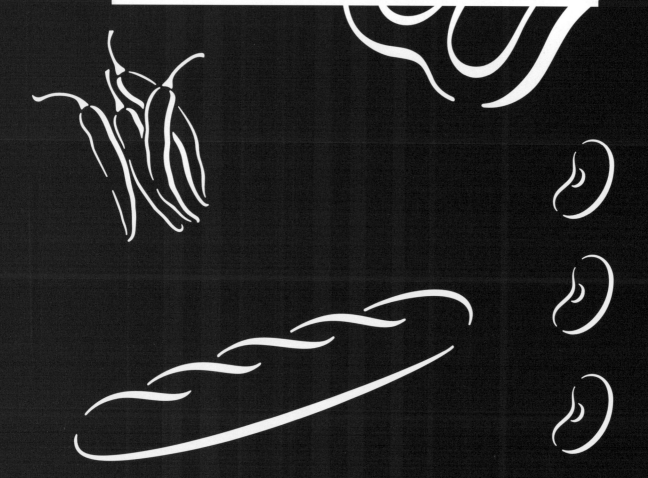

STARTERS

Cheese, Potato, and Rice Galette with Smoked Ham

3 pounds Yukon Gold or Russet potatoes, peeled and quartered

6 ounces (approximately 4 1/2 cups)
cooked wild rice mix (see sidebar)

3 ounces Gruyère or Swiss cheese, grated

3 ounces Parmesan cheese, grated

3 ounces smoked Gouda cheese, grated

6 ounces smoked ham, thinly sliced into
1/2-inch squares

1/2 cup thinly sliced scallions, green parts
only, or chives

1/2 teaspoon freshly ground pepper

Salmon caviar and sour cream,
for garnish (optional)

SERVES 6

This galette is especially easy to make when you have leftover rice. Otherwise, prepare a box of wild rice mix according to the manufacturer's instuctions. There is no need to add salt to the pancakes because the ham and cheeses are quite salty. If you don't have a 13-inch pan, use two 10-inch pans.

✱ Fill a large pot with cold water, add the potatoes, and bring to boil. Drain right away (do not cook) and run under cold water to stop the cooking. Drain again and set aside to cool.

✱ When the potatoes are cool enough to handle, place in the bowl of an electric mixer fitted with a grating blade, and grate. Transfer the potatoes to a bowl and gently fold in the cooked wild rice mix, the cheeses, ham, scallions, and pepper.

✱ Preheat the oven to 375° F.

✱ Place an ovenproof, nonstick 13-inch skillet over medium-high heat, and let the pan get hot. Add the oil and then, using a wooden spoon, scrape the mixture into the skillet. Spread the batter evenly so that it creates a flat layer that reaches to the sides of the pan. Cook over medium-high heat for 8 to 10 minutes, or until the bottom of the galette is slightly browned. (If the galette begins to stick, shake the pan and scrape the batter off the bottom and reincorporate it into the mixture in order to form one solid pancake.) Place the skillet in the oven and finish cooking for 30 to 35 minutes, or until the bottom of the galette is golden brown.

✱ Run a long spatula underneath and around the sides of the galette to ensure that it is not stuck to the pan. Place a serving plate on top of the skillet and slowly flip the pan over, toward you.

✱ To serve, cut into 6 wedges and garnish each wedge with a dollop of sour cream and caviar, if desired.

Grilled Mozzarella with Tomato Vinegar

SERVES 4

This recipe, by Michael Chiarello, provides easy instructions on how to make your own flavored vinegar. Use the leftover vinegar as a sauce for fried foods or tossed in pasta salads. Reprinted from *Flavored Vinegars* (Chronicle Books).

Tomato Vinegar

1 tablespoon olive oil

1 tablespoon minced garlic

1 cup peeled, seeded, and chopped vine-ripe tomatoes or good quality canned tomatoes

1/4 cup plus 1 cup water

4 ounces oil-packed sun-dried tomatoes, rehydrated in water

Salt and freshly ground pepper

1/2 cup champagne vinegar

2 tablespoons finely chopped fresh basil (optional)

4 very large romaine leaves

8 ounces fresh mozzarella cheese, cut into 4 equal pieces

Salt and freshly ground pepper

1 1/2 ounces dried prosciutto, diced

1 tablespoon extra-virgin olive oil

6 tablespoons tomato vinegar (see left), or more to taste

2 tablespoons Spanish or French extra-virgin olive oil

1 large bunch arugula, watercress, or other crisp, spicy green

2 tablespoons freshly grated Parmesan cheese

✱ To make the tomato vinegar, heat the oil in a small sauté pan over medium-high heat until almost smoking. Add garlic and sauté, moving the pan off and on the heat to regulate the temperature, until light brown. Add tomatoes, 1/4 cup water, and bring to a boil. Reduce heat to medium and simmer until thick. Add sun-dried tomatoes and cook until they soften, approximately 3 minutes. Season with salt and pepper. Purée tomato mixture in a blender. Add vinegar and thin with the remaining water, if necessary. Pulse in the basil, if desired. Adjust the seasoning with salt, pepper, and vinegar. Pour into a bowl or pitcher, then transfer to a clean, wide-mouth bottle or jar and cover with a nonmetallic lid. The tomato vinegar will keep in the refrigerator up to 1 week. Makes 2 cups of tomato vinegar.

✱ Bring a pot of salted water to a boil. Blanch the romaine leaves until they turn bright green and the central ribs are just tender enough to bend, approximately 30 seconds. Remove and immediately plunge the romaine into ice water to stop the cooking. Drain and pat dry.

✱ Prepare a grill or preheat the broiler. Lay the romaine leaves out on a clean work surface, rib-side down. Cut out the widest part of the central rib by making a triangular cut at the base of each leaf. Place a square of cheese in the middle of each leaf. Season with salt and pepper. Sprinkle each with approximately 1 tablespoon prosciutto. Make a neat package by folding the leaves around the cheese like an envelope, ending seam-side down. Brush each package with olive oil.

✳ In a bowl, combine the tomato vinegar and olive oil. Add the arugula or other greens and toss lightly to dress. Taste and add more vinegar, salt, and pepper, if necessary. Arrange the greens evenly in a wreathlike pattern on each of the 4 plates. Sprinkle the greens with some Parmesan.

✳ Place the cheese packages on the grill or put in a preheated broiler approximately 4 inches from the heat. Cook 2 to 3 minutes, then turn over. Cook for another 1 to 2 minutes, or just until the cheese begins to melt and the packages are soft to the touch and lightly brown. Do not let the cheese get too hot or it will toughen as it cools.

✳ To serve, set the grilled mozzarella in center of each salad plate. Serve immediately.

Nutty Pineapple Nibbles

6 celery stalks

1/4 cup canned crushed pineapple, drained

1/2 cup soft light cream cheese

2 tablespoons creamy peanut butter

1 tablespoon honey

1/4 cup raisins or dried fruit bits

1/4 teaspoon hot pepper sauce (optional)

3 tablespoons finely crushed dry-roasted nuts

✳ Rinse the celery, then trim off the leafy parts, and cut into 10-inch pieces.

✳ In a medium-sized bowl, combine the drained pineapple, cream cheese, peanut butter, and honey. Stir with a rubber spatula until well mixed. Stir in the raisins or fruit bits and hot sauce, if desired.

✳ Using a table knife, fill the groove of each celery stalk with the cheese mixture. Sprinkle the crushed nuts over the stalks.

SERVES 10

It's important to get kids into the kitchen to help them learn good cooking skills and healthy eating habits. These after-school snacks are easy and fun to prepare. Reprinted from *Kid's Cookbook* (American Heart Association).

Black Bean Nachos

SERVES 12 TO 16

What we call *nachos* in Tex-Mex cooking are actually called *tostados* in Mexico: toasted tortilla chips with a topping. There are several components to this version created by Martha Rose Schulman, but the refried beans can be prepared up to 3 days in advance and kept in the refrigerator. The *salsa fresca* is simple to make and is best prepared 15 minutes before serving. Reprinted from *Mexican Light* (Bantam Books).

Refried Black Beans

1 pound dried black beans or pintos, washed and picked over to remove any dirt or stones

1 onion, chopped

4 large garlic cloves, minced, or more to taste

2 to 3 teaspoons salt, or more to taste

2 large fresh epazote sprigs or 2 heaping tablespoons fresh cilantro leaves

2 tablespoons canola oil

1 tablespoon ground cumin

2 teaspoons pure ground mild or medium-hot chili powder

12 corn tortillas, cut into quarters or sixths

Salsa Fresca

1 to 1 1/4 pounds (4 medium or 2 large) tomatoes, finely chopped

1/2 small red onion, minced

2 to 3 jalapeño or serrano chilies, or more to taste (seeded and minced for a milder salsa)

1/4 cup chopped fresh cilantro, or more to taste

1 to 2 teaspoons balsamic vinegar, rice wine vinegar, or fresh lime juice (optional)

1/2 teaspoon salt, or to taste

1/4 pound *queso fresco*, *cotija*, or feta, crumbled, for garnish

✳ To make the refried beans, soak the beans in 6 cups water overnight, or for at least 6 hours. Drain the beans, then rinse with hot water and drain again.

✳ In a heavy-bottomed pot, combine the beans, onion, and 2 quarts fresh water, or enough to cover the beans by an inch. Bring to a boil, skim off any foam, and add 2 garlic cloves. Reduce the heat, cover, and simmer for 1 hour. Add the remaining garlic, the salt, and epazote, cover, and simmer for another hour, or until the beans are soft and their liquid is thick and soupy. Add salt to taste if necessary. Remove from heat.

✳ Drain the beans, reserving approximately 1 cup liquid. Mash half the beans coarsely in a food processor or with a bean or potato masher. (Do not purée them.) Stir the mashed beans back into the pot. Heat the oil in a large heavy nonstick skillet over medium heat and add the cumin and ground chili. Cook, stirring, over medium heat for about a minute, until the spices begin to sizzle and their pungent aromas are released. Raise the heat to medium-high and add the bean mixture. Fry the beans, stirring and mashing often, until they thicken and begin to get aromatic and crusty on the bottom. Stir up the crust each time it forms on the bottom of the pan and mix in with the beans. Cook for approximately 20 minutes, stirring often and mashing the beans with a bean masher or the back of your spoon. The beans should be thick but not dry. Add some of the reserved liquid if they seem too dry.

✳ Taste the refried beans and adjust the salt. Set aside in the pan if you're serving within a few hours. They will continue to dry out, so make sure you keep adding the remaining bean liquid. Otherwise, transfer the beans to a lightly oiled baking dish and cover with foil.

✳ Meanwhile, prepare the *salsa fresca:* Combine all the ingredients in a medium bowl and mix well. Let sit for at least 15 minutes before serving. (You should have 2 cups of salsa.)

✳ To toast the tortilla chips, preheat the oven to 325° F. Place the tortilla pieces on a baking sheet and bake for 20 to 30 minutes, until light brown and crisp, shaking the baking sheet every 10 minutes. Transfer to a rack to cool. Alternatively, to microwave the chips, place 6 to 20 pieces on a plate or on the plate in your microwave. Microwave on High for 1 minute. If the pieces are not crisp and are just beginning to brown, microwave for another 20 to 30 seconds, until crisp. Cool on a rack or in a basket.

✳ To serve the nachos, reheat the refried beans and spread a spoonful on each tortilla chip. Sprinkle on some cheese and dot with *salsa fresca*.

Assorted Crostini and Toppings

SERVES 4

This colorful appetizer is a breeze to prepare, especially if the pesto, tapenade, and sun-dried tomato spreads are made ahead. The toppings can be prepared and then stored in covered containers in the refrigerator for approximately 1 week. Reprinted from *Casual Occasions Cookbook* (Weldon Owen).

¹/₂ French baguette or 1 loaf country-style French or Italian bread approximately 3 to 4 inches in diameter

¹/₄ cup pesto (recipe follows)

¹/₄ cup tapenade (recipe follows)

¹/₄ cup sun-dried tomato spread (recipe follows)

24 small or 12 large slices mozzarella or fontina cheese

✱ Preheat the broiler. Cut the baguette diagonally into 24 slices each approximately ¼ inch thick. If using country-style loaf, cut 12 slices each approximately ¼ inch thick. Arrange the bread slices on a baking sheet and broil, turning once, until lightly golden, approximately 2 minutes on each side. Remove from the broiler but leave the broiler on.

✱ If using baguette slices, spread 8 toasted bread slices with an equal amount of the pesto. If using the larger bread slices, divide the pesto evenly among 4 slices. Then divide the tapenade and the sun-dried tomato spread evenly among the remaining toasted bread slices. Place a slice of cheese on top, using the size that matches the bread slices.

✱ Return the slices to the broiler and broil until the cheese melts. Serve immediately.

Pesto

2 cups firmly packed fresh basil leaves

2 teaspoons minced garlic

2 to 3 tablespoons pine nuts or walnuts

¹/₂ to 1 teaspoon salt, or to taste

¹/₂ teaspoon freshly ground pepper

1 cup olive oil

¹/₂ cup freshly grated Parmesan cheese

✱ To make the pesto, combine the basil, garlic, pine nuts, salt, and pepper in a food processor fitted with the metal blade or in a blender. Process until well combined. Add ½ cup of the olive oil in a slow, steady stream and purée using short off-on pulses. Stir between the pulses to blend well. Add the remaining ½ cup oil and the cheese and process to form a thick purée. Do not overprocess; you want the mixture to have a little texture. Taste and adjust the salt and pepper. Transfer to a covered container and store in the refrigerator for up to 1 week. Makes 3 cups.

Sun-Dried Tomato Spread

1 cup chopped, strained oil-packed
   sun-dried tomatoes (oil reserved)
4 to 6 tablespoons coarsely chopped
   roasted bell pepper or pimentos
   (approximately 1 medium pepper,
   roasted)

1 tablespoon minced garlic
4 tablespoons fresh basil leaves
   (optional)
Pinch of cayenne pepper (optional)
Extra-virgin olive oil

✳ To make the sun-dried tomato spread, combine the tomatoes, roasted red bell pepper, garlic, basil, and cayenne pepper, if desired, in a food processor fitted with the metal blade or in a blender. Measure the reserved oil from the tomatoes. Add enough extra-virgin olive oil to measure ¼ cup. Add to the food processor or blender and purée until smooth. Transfer to a covered container and store in the refrigerator for up to 1 week. Makes 1½ cups.

Tapenade

1 cup pitted Niçoise or Kalamata olives
2 tablespoons capers, rinsed and
   drained
1 tablespoon minced garlic
2 teaspoons chopped, drained
   anchovy fillet

¹/₂ teaspoon freshly ground pepper
6 tablespoons extra-virgin olive oil
Finely grated zest of 1 lemon or orange
   (optional)
2 tablespoons Cognac (optional)

✳ To make the tapenade, combine the olives, capers, garlic, anchovy, pepper, olive oil, and the zest and Cognac, if desired, in a food processor fitted with the metal blade or in a blender; purée until smooth. Transfer to a covered container and store in the refrigerator for up to 2 weeks. Makes 1½ cups.

Sourdough White Bread

**MAKES 1 LOAF
OR 4 BAGUETTES**

Lora Brody provides
this easy and
forgiving bread
recipe, which is made
in the bread machine.
The secret ingredient
is the Sourdough
Bread Enhancement
Formula™, which is
available at gourmet
food shops nationally.
Reprinted from
*Pizza, Focaccia, Filled
& Flat Breads from
Your Bread Machine*
(William Morrow
& Co.).

1 tablespoon instant active dry yeast
3 cups all-purpose unbleached
   white flour
1 ½ teaspoons salt
1 tablespoon sugar
6 tablespoons Sourdough Bread
   Enhancement Formula™
8 to 10 ounces water

Egg Wash

1 egg
1 tablespoon water

✳ Place all the ingredients except the egg wash in a bread machine, mixer, or food processor. Knead, mix, or process, adding additional water or flour as necessary to form a smooth, supple ball of dough after the first few minutes of kneading.

✳ If you are using the bread machine and wish to bake the bread in the machine, program it for White or Basic Bread. If you wish to form the dough by hand, then program the machine for Dough or Manual.

✳ Using the food processor or mixer, knead the dough until it is supple, smooth, and elastic, then allow it to rise, covered in a warm place until double in bulk.

✳ **To make a loaf,** punch down the dough and place in a well-greased loaf pan. Cover and allow to rise until almost double in bulk.

✳ Preheat the oven to 450° F. Bake the risen dough for 20 minutes, then lower the temperature to 375° F and bake for an additional 10 to 15 minutes, or until the bottom of the loaf sounds hollow when tapped. Let cool on a wire rack before slicing.

✳ **To make baguettes,** punch down the dough and divide it into 4 equal pieces. Roll each piece out into approximately a 4- x 2½-inch rope. Place the ropes in lightly greased baguette pans, or 3 inches apart on a baking sheet lightly oiled and then dusted with cornmeal. Cover with oiled plastic wrap or a damp towel and allow to rise until almost double in volume.

✳ Preheat the oven to 450° F. Using a sharp knife, make ¼-inch-deep diagonal slashes at 2-inch intervals on the tops of the loaves. To make the egg wash, beat the egg with the water. Brush the top of the dough with the egg wash and bake for 18 to 20 minutes. Slide the baguettes directly onto the oven rack and bake an additional 5 minutes. Let cool on a wire rack before slicing.

Prepared Minced Garlic

1 head garlic   Olive oil

MAKES 1/2 CUP MINCED GARLIC

❋ To remove the cloves from the bulb, place the bulb on a flat work surface, pointed-side down, and gently push on the whole bulb, moving it from side to side, until the bulb loosens and the cloves, still in the skin, separate.

❋ Place the individual cloves on the work surface and, using the flat side of a chef's knife, push down on the cloves, crushing them. Remove the skins.

❋ Place the peeled garlic cloves in a food processor fitted the metal blade and pulse until minced, but not puréed. Add just enough oil to moisten the garlic and keep it from drying out. It should look like wet sand.

❋ If you prefer to make a smaller batch of minced garlic, finely mince a few cloves of garlic with a chef's knife, transfer to a small cup, and stir in enough oil to cover. As a rule of thumb, 2 cloves of garlic, minced, plus ¼ teaspoon of oil equals approximately 1 teaspoon of prepared minced garlic.

❋ Transfer the prepared minced garlic to a clean jar with a tight-fitting lid and store in the refrigerator for a few days, or up to 1 week.

Homemade or store-bought minced garlic is a welcome convenience in the kitchen, especially for those who cook with a lot of garlic. However, garlic stored in oil has a short shelf life and must be refrigerated to prevent harmful bacteria and mold from forming. Prepared minced garlic should be thrown out after 1 week.

Tomato Bread Soup

1 tablespoon olive oil

6 cloves garlic, minced, plus ³/₄ tea-
    spoon oil, or 3 teaspoons prepared
    minced garlic (see page 17)

1 teaspoon sugar

1 teaspoon chili powder

1 (14 ¹/₂-ounce) can diced tomatoes

1 (46-ounce) can tomato juice

Salt and freshly ground pepper

1 (15-ounce) can cannellini beans,
    rinsed and drained

Croutons

1 loaf Italian or French bread,
    cut diagonally into 18 slices
    approximately 1 inch thick

2 tablespoons olive oil

Garlic powder

¹/₂ cup freshly grated Parmesan cheese

Paprika

Cayenne pepper

1 cup loosely packed fresh basil leaves,
    cut into ¹/₈-inch-thick strips

SERVES 6

This delicious soup
will make you forget
about the canned
tomato soup of
your childhood. In
fact, when served
with white cannellini
beans and fresh,
crisp croutons,
it's elegant enough
for a dinner party.
Remember to slice
the bread on
the diagonal for an
attractive crouton.

✳ Heat the oil in a large stockpot over low heat. Add the garlic, sugar, and chili powder and sauté until aromatic, approximately 1 to 2 minutes. Add the tomatoes, tomato
juice, salt, and pepper and simmer for 5 minutes. Just before serving, add the beans to
the soup to warm through.

✳ To make the croutons, preheat the oven to 375° F and brush the bread slices with
olive oil. Sprinkle each slice with some garlic powder, Parmesan cheese, paprika, and
cayenne. Bake in the oven until golden brown, approximately 5 minutes. Cut each
crouton in half.

✳ To serve, ladle the soup into 6 bowls. Place 6 crouton halves in the center of each
bowl and garnish with the basil.

Southwestern Corn Chowder with Chicken

SERVES 6

The inclusion of potatoes is what makes this one-pot soup considered a chowder. Dredging the chicken in flour before adding it to the soup adds flavor and gives the soup a thicker, creamier consistency.

Flour, for dredging

1 1/2 pounds boneless and skinless chicken breast, cut diagonally into 1/2-inch thick strips

2 tablespoons olive oil

1/4 teaspoon cayenne pepper

1 teaspoon chili powder

1/2 tablespoon dried oregano

1/2 tablespoon olive oil

4 cloves garlic, minced, plus 1/2 teaspoon oil, or 2 teaspoons prepared minced garlic (see page 17)

1 red onion, cut into 1/2-inch dice

1 Spanish onion, cut into 1/2-inch dice

2 red peppers, cut into 3/4-inch dice

1 jalapeño chili, minced

1 potato, peeled and cut into 1/2-inch dice

3 cups chicken stock (homemade or low-sodium canned)

1 (11-ounce) can corn, drained (or 1 1/4 cups frozen corn)

1 (15-ounce) can hominy, rinsed and drained

1 1/2 teaspoons salt, or to taste

2 limes, each cut into six wedges (optional)

1/4 cup scallions, green parts only, thinly sliced (optional)

✱ Place the flour in a large bowl. Dredge the chicken strips in the flour, shaking off any excess flour. Place a large pan over medium-high heat and allow the pan to heat up. Add the oil, then add the chicken to the pan and sauté until golden brown.

✱ Remove the chicken from pan and set aside. Add the cayenne, chili powder, and oregano and toast over low heat for a few minutes to allow the flavors to be released. Add the garlic and sauté over medium heat until golden brown, approximately 1 to 2 minutes. Add the onions and peppers and continue to sauté until the onions turn golden, approximately 5 minutes. Add the potatoes and chicken stock and simmer for 5 minutes.

✱ Stir in the corn and the hominy and place the chicken on top of the soup. (Do not mix the chicken into the soup or it may overcook or get mushy.) Simmer over low heat for 10 minutes, or until the potatoes are tender. Add salt to taste.

✱ To serve, evenly distribute the chicken between 6 bowls and ladle the soup on top. Garnish with wedges of lime and sliced scallions, if desired.

Caramelized Onion Soup

Caramelized Onions

6 Vidalia onions (approximately 2 ¹/₂ pounds; approximately 3 to 4 inches in diameter), stem and root ends sliced off, peeled, and left whole

¹/₂ cup (8 tablespoons) unsalted butter

Soup

3 to 4 cups caramelized onions (from left)

3 cups onion cooking liquid from the Crock-Pot

3 cups low- or no-salt vegetable, chicken, or beef broth

Salt and freshly ground pepper

SERVES 8

Caramelized onions, slowly cooked in a Crock-Pot are the secret to this rich soup created by Lora Brody. You can easily substitute Spanish or even regular yellow onions for the Vidalias. To make a nonfat version of this soup, eliminate the butter and cook the onions in one cup of broth. Reprinted from *The Kitchen Survival Guide* (William Morrow & Co.).

✴ To make the caramelized onions, place the whole onions and butter in a Crock-Pot and cook on Low until the onions are deep golden brown in color and very soft, anywhere from 12 to 24 hours. (Different Crock-Pots will take different amounts of time, but it is almost impossible to overcook the onions.) Set aside 3 to 4 cups for the soup and reserve the extra onions for another use (such as Sourdough Pizza with Potatoes and Caramelized Onions on page 49).

✴ To make the soup, combine the 3 to 4 cups caramelized onions, the onion cooking liquid, and the broth in a large pot, and warm over low heat until thoroughly heated. Season to taste with salt and pepper.

✴ To serve, evenly distribute the onions among 8 bowls and ladle the soup on top.

Hunter-Style Mushroom Ragoût on Croutons

1 ½ cups water

1 ounce dried shiitake mushrooms

1 ounce dried chanterelle mushrooms

1 ounce dried crimini mushrooms

4 garlic cloves, minced, plus ½ teaspoon oil, or 2 teaspoons prepared minced garlic (see page 17)

½ tablespoon olive oil

1 large onion, cut into large dice

1 ½ cups fresh white button mushrooms, quartered

½ cup port wine

¾ cup half-and-half

1 large tomato, peeled and cut into small dice

1 tablespoon lemon juice

Salt and freshly ground pepper

Croutons

1 loaf French bread, cut diagonally into 12 slices approximately ¾ inch thick

1 tablespoon olive oil, or more as needed

1 ½ tablespoons chopped fresh parsley, for garnish

1 ½ tablespoons chopped fresh chives, for garnish

SERVES 6

This earthy, rustic stew derives its concentrated flavor from the combination of wild and dried mushrooms. The ragoût is also wonderful served on top of filet mignon for a main course.

✱ Bring 1½ cups water to a boil in a small saucepan. Add the dried mushrooms, remove from the heat, and let soak for 30 minutes. Strain the mushrooms and reserve the liquid.

✱ In large skillet, sauté the garlic in oil over low heat until aromatic, approximately 1 to 2 minutes. Add the onion and sauté until translucent, approximately 3 to 5 minutes. Add the fresh and rehydrated mushrooms and sauté for another 2 minutes.

✱ Add the reserved mushroom soaking liquid and port to the skillet. Cook over medium-high heat until the liquid reduces in volume by one-half, approximately 6 to 8 minutes. Add the half-and-half, tomato, and lemon juice and bring to a simmer. Continue cooking until the mixture is thickened. Season with salt and pepper to taste.

✱ While the sauce is reducing, prepare the croutons. Preheat the oven to 375° F. Brush the bread slices with the oil and place on baking pan. Bake in oven until golden brown, approximately 12 minutes.

✱ To serve, spoon the mushroom ragoût into a serving bowl or onto individual plates and place the croutons alongside. Garnish with the parsely and chives.

Vegetable and Chorizo Frittata with Tomato-Basil Chutney

SERVES 4

This frittata is a star attraction at the world-famous DIVA restaurant in the Metropolitan Hotel in Vancouver, B.C. and comes from their executive chef and Culinary Olympic winner, Michael Noble. If you're not planning to go to Vancouver, try this dish, which doesn't require flipping, at home.

Tomato-Basil Chutney

1/2 red onion, finely diced

1/2 red bell pepper, diced

1 teaspoon olive oil

3 tablespoons raspberry vinegar

1 tablespoon sugar

2 tomatoes, blanched, peeled, seeded and diced

2 teaspoons chopped fresh basil

Salt and freshly ground pepper

Frittata

4 tablespoons olive oil

1 potato, peeled, boiled until tender, and diced

1/2 medium onion, diced

1 red bell pepper, cut into thin strips

1 yellow bell pepper, cut into thin strips

8 ounces chorizo sausage, thinly sliced

2 cloves garlic, crushed or minced

12 eggs

6 ounces Monterey Jack cheese, grated

8 tablespoons tomato-basil chutney (see left), for garnish

4 sprigs fresh basil, for garnish

✳ To make the tomato-basil chutney, in a medium saucepan, sauté the onion and the red pepper in olive oil over medium heat. Add the raspberry vinegar and sugar. Cook over medium heat until the liquid has reduced in volume by three-quarters, approximately 3 to 4 minutes. Add the tomato and cook 15 to 20 minutes, or until most of the liquid has evaporated. Add the basil and season to taste with salt and pepper. Keep at room temperature if serving right away or refrigerate overnight. Makes 1 cup chutney.

✳ To make the frittata in a 12-inch nonstick frying pan, sauté the potatoes in 2 tablespoons of olive oil over medium heat until slightly brown, approximately 5 to 7 minutes. Add the onion and sauté for 2 minutes. Add the peppers, chorizo, and garlic and sauté for an additional 2 minutes, or until the onion and peppers become slightly browned. Remove from the pan and set aside.

✳ In a small bowl, beat 3 eggs. Heat an 8-inch nonstick frying pan over high heat with 1/2 tablespoon olive oil until lightly smoking. Add one-fourth of the vegetable and chorizo mixture and sauté for a minute or two. Pour the eggs over the mixture and stir vigorously with a spatula until the eggs start to set. Reduce the heat to low and let the eggs cook until the frittata comes loose from the sides of the pan when shaken.

✳ Preheat the broiler. Sprinkle the cheese over the top. Place frying pan in the broiler for a few minutes to firm up the top of the frittata. The frittata should slide easily out of the pan with the help of a spatula.

✳ Repeat the procedure for each of the 3 other frittatas.

✳ To serve, top each frittata with 2 tablespoons tomato-basil chutney and garnish with a fresh sprig of basil.

Breakfast Cobbler with Sausage, Apples, Onions, and Cheddar Cheese

1 pound breakfast sausage
3 medium onions, cut into large dice
3 medium-sized Golden Delicious apples,
    cut into large chunks

Cobbler Batter

2 teaspoons vegetable oil
1/2 cup sour cream, low-fat preferred
1 egg

1/2 cup yellow cornmeal
1/2 cup all-purpose flour
1/2 teaspoon baking powder
1 teaspoon baking soda
1 teaspoon salt
1/2 teaspoon freshly ground pepper
1/2 cup buttermilk

1 cup Cheddar cheese, grated

SERVES 4

Here's a unique and delicious brunch casserole. With the meat, potatoes, and cheese all combined into one dish, you might call it "one-stop" eating. Stick to the old-fashioned breakfast sausages for this recipe, and avoid some of the flavored sausages which can have a high water content or artificial flavorings.

✳ Cut the sausage in large 1½-inch pieces. In large skillet, sauté the sausage over medium heat for approximately 10 minutes, until it begins to brown. Add the onions and apples to the pan and sauté until soft and golden, approximately 5 minutes, and set aside.

✳ To make the cobbler batter, place the oil, sour cream, and egg in a bowl and beat together with an electric mixer or by hand. In separate bowl, mix the dry ingredients together. Add the dry ingredients alternately with the buttermilk to the egg mixture until fully incorporated.

✳ Preheat the oven to 375° F. (If using a glass baking dish, bake at 350° F.) Grease a 9- x 12-inch baking dish and pour the filling mixture into the bottom of the dish. Evenly pour the batter on top of the filling and sprinkle with the cheese. Bake in the oven for 25 minutes, or until the top is golden brown and the batter is cooked through. (A toothpick inserted in the center should come out dry.)

✳ Let cool slightly before serving.

Whole Wheat Pancakes with Blueberry Compote

Blueberry Compote

3 tablespoons sugar

1 tablespoon raspberry vinegar

1/4 cup orange juice

Zest from 1 orange, finely chopped

2 tablespoons port wine (optional)

2 cups (1 pound) fresh blueberries

Pancakes

1 cup all-purpose flour

1/2 cup whole wheat flour

3 teaspoons baking powder

1/2 teaspoon salt

3 tablespoons sugar

1 egg

3 tablespoons vegetable oil

1 1/2 cups milk, or more as needed

1/4 teaspoon vanilla extract

Blueberry Compote (see left), warmed

4 sprigs fresh mint, for garnish

SERVES 4

This is one of the most popular breakfast items at Vancouver's DIVA restaurant. Star chef Michael Noble confesses that he did not invent the recipe, but "borrowed" it from his mother. If you can't find fresh blueberries, substitute frozen blueberries.

✱ To make the blueberry compote, place a small saucepan over medium heat. When the pan is medium hot, slowly add the sugar a sprinkle at a time while stirring constantly to melt. Continue cooking until the sugar turns to caramel.

✱ Pour in the raspberry vinegar and orange juice and deglaze the pan, scraping up the bits stuck to the pan. Add the zest and port, if desired, and continue to cook over medium heat until almost all the liquid has evaporated and the mixture starts to get thick and syrupy.

✱ Add the blueberries, bring to a simmer, and cook until the berries soften slightly, approximately 5 minutes. (If the compote is too runny, thicken it slightly with 1 teaspoon cornstarch dissolved in 2 teaspoons orange juice.) Serve warm.

✱ To make the pancakes, in a large bowl combine flours, baking powder, salt and sugar. In a separate bowl, whisk together the egg, oil, milk, and vanilla. Add the wet ingredients to the dry and mix to incorporate well. Let rest for 5 minutes.

✱ Pour 1/4 cup of batter onto a nonstick griddle or frying pan (do not add oil) and cook over medium heat. Cook until the edges of the pancakes are dry and small bubbles have formed on top, approximately 1 1/2 minutes; then flip with a spatula. Transfer to a 250° F oven to keep warm while repeating the procedure with the remaining batter.

✱ To serve, top the warm pancakes with 1/4 cup warm blueberry compote per person, and garnish with a sprig of fresh mint.

SALADS, SANDWICHES AND SIDES

Blood Oranges and Celery Root with Mustard Vinaigrette

3 blood oranges

Mustard Vinaigrette
1 tablespoon fruit-flavored vinegar, such as peach or raspberry, or mild white wine vinegar
$1/8$ teaspoon salt

Freshly ground pepper
2 teaspoons Dijon mustard
2 teaspoons honey
$1/3$ cup extra-virgin olive oil

1 celery root (approximately 1 pound)
8 to 10 ounces mixed salad greens

✴ Peel the oranges, cutting away all of the white pith and outer membrane. Holding each orange over a bowl and using a sharp, thin-bladed knife, cut along both sides of each segment, against the membrane, to release the whole segments into the bowl. Discard any seeds. Set aside.

✴ To make the vinaigrette, in a small bowl combine the vinegar, salt, and pepper to taste. Using a small whisk, stir until the salt dissolves. Add the mustard and honey and whisk until blended. Taste and adjust the seasonings. Pour half of the vinaigrette into a medium bowl.

✴ Using a sharp knife, peel the celery root and shred on the medium holes of a hand-held shredder. Immediately place in the medium bowl holding the mustard vinaigrette. Mix well. (This step can be done up to 1 hour before serving.)

✴ To serve, divide the salad greens among 6 salad plates, arranging them in a ring on each. Divide the shredded celery root among the plates, placing it in the center. Arrange the orange segments on the greens and serve at once.

SERVES 6

Blood oranges and celery root are found in the market in the cool months, making this an ideal course for a Christmas meal. The vinaigrette, oranges, and lettuces can be prepared up to 4 hours in advance and refrigerated separately. Reprinted from *Casual Occasions Cookbook* (Weldon Owen).

Grilled Bread Salad with Roasted Peppers and Cherry Tomatoes

1 (10-ounce) loaf fresh or day-old
  crusty Italian bread

1/4 cup olive oil, preferably extra-virgin

3 red bell peppers, cut into 1-inch-
  thick strips

2 cups cherry tomatoes, halved

1/2 cup pure maple syrup

2 teaspoons fresh lemon juice

1 teaspoon dried oregano

2 bunches arugula, coarse stems
  removed

1 Belgian endive, leaves separated

SERVES 4

This is a variation on
the classic bread salad,
called *panzanella* in
Italy, named *Shalada
del Khobz Yabess* in
Morocco, and *Fattoush*
in Lebanon. To boost
the smoky flavor of
foods that require
only a short grilling
time, as is the case
with this bread salad,
keep the lid of the
barbecue closed.

✳ Several hours before serving, slice the fresh bread in half lengthwise, then slice each half lengthwise into 3 or 4 long "fingers." Let the bread stand uncovered for several hours to dry out. If using day-old bread, skip this step.

✳ Prepare a grill. Brush the bread all over with some of the oil and place on the grill over medium-high heat, turning often, until lightly browned all over, approximately 4 to 6 minutes. Cut each piece of bread into 4 elongated cubes. Set aside.

✳ In a medium bowl, combine the red peppers and cherry tomatoes. Add the maple syrup and toss. Add 2 tablespoons of the olive oil, lemon juice, and oregano and toss again. Let the vegetables marinate for 20 to 30 minutes.

✳ Place the peppers and tomatoes in a grill basket, reserving the marinade. Place on the grill over medium-high heat and cook 8 to 12 minutes, or until lightly charred, turning carefully every few minutes.

✳ In a bowl, combine the grilled vegetables, bread cubes, and reserved marinade and toss lightly.

✳ To serve, line 4 individual salad plates or one large platter with the arugula and endive leaves. Arrange the grilled bread, peppers, and tomatoes on top.

Vegetable Salad with Crisp Sesame Seed Pancakes

SERVES 6

The sesame pancakes provide a flavorful and wonderful partner to this vegetable salad. The secret ingredient in the pancakes is Cream of Wheat™, which makes a surprisingly delicious departure from your everyday pancake.

Sesame Pancakes

1 cup water

1/4 teaspoon kosher salt

3 tablespoons Cream of Wheat™ (not instant)

4 tablespoons sesame seeds

1/2 tablespoon olive oil

1 cup cauliflower florets

1 cup sugar snap peas

1 cup carrots, cut into large dice

1 cup broccoli florets

1 large red pepper, sliced into thin strips

2 tomatoes, peeled, seeded, and cut into large dice

Salad Dressing

3 tablespoons sesame oil

3 tablespoons rice wine vinegar

2 tablespoons honey

2 tablespoons Italian parsley, chopped

1 small bunch chives, thinly sliced

1/4 teaspoon fresh ground pepper

✳ To make the sesame pancakes, in a large saucepan, boil the water and salt. Whisk in the Cream of Wheat and 2 tablespoons of the sesame seeds. Boil for 3 minutes, stirring constantly.

✳ Line a small baking sheet with plastic wrap. Spoon the wheat mixture onto the baking sheet into 12 equal mounds. Cover with plastic wrap and pat each pile into a 1/3-inch thick pancake approximately 2 1/2 to 3 inches in diameter. Place the sheet in the refrigerator or freezer to cool.

✳ While the wheat mixture is cooling, blanch all the vegetables (except the tomatoes) separately in boiling water, each time cooking the vegetables until just al dente, then removing and running under cold water to stop the cooking.

✳ To make the salad dressing, place all ingredients in a food processor fitted with a metal blade or a blender and blend thoroughly.

✳ In a large bowl, toss the cooked vegetables and the tomatoes with the dressing and set aside.

✳ Remove the wheat patties from the refrigerator and dredge in the remaining 2 tablespoons sesame seeds to coat all over.

✳ In a hot nonstick pan over medium heat, sauté patties in olive oil until light golden brown on both sides, approximately 2 to 3 minutes on each side.

✳ To serve, place approximately 1 cup of the mixed vegetables on each plate and top with 2 pancakes.

Jerk Chicken Sandwich with Grilled Pineapple and Colby Cheese

SERVES 6

If you prefer,
you can substitute
Cheddar or Jack
cheese for the Colby.
You could also broil
the pineapple instead
of grilling it.

Marinade

1 tablespoon olive or vegetable oil

1 cup ketchup

1/2 teaspoon garlic powder

1 teaspoon dried basil

1 tablespoon jerk seasoning or
    Jamaican spice blend

1 tablespoon lime or lemon juice

6 boneless and skinless chicken breast
    halves (approximately 4 ounces each)

12 slices (1/4 inch thick) fresh or
    canned pineapple

6 ounces Colby cheese, cut into 12 slices

6 large lettuce leaves, for garnish

6 sesame-seeded hoagie rolls (or any
    sandwich bread)

✱ Mix all the marinade ingredients together in a large bowl. Reserve one-third of the marinade for a sandwich spread. Toss the chicken in the remaining marinade, then place the chicken on a rimmed baking sheet. Set in the refrigerator and marinate for 20 minutes.

✱ While the chicken is marinating, prepare a grill or place a grill pan over high heat.

✱ Brush the pineapple slices with some of the reserved marinade and grill until they turn golden brown and soften slightly, approximately 5 minutes on each side, depending on the thickness.

✱ Preheat the oven to 325° F. Remove the chicken from the marinade, shaking off any excess, place on a baking sheet, and bake for approximately 20 minutes, or until the chicken is done.

✱ Leave the oven on and place the rolls on a sheet pan and toast for 3 to 4 minutes until lightly brown and warmed through. Remove the rolls from the oven and transfer to a cutting board. Brush each roll with some of the reserved marinade. Arrange 1 chicken breast on each roll top, cover with 2 pineapple slices, and then top with 2 slices of cheese. Turn on the broiler, place the sandwiches on the baking sheet, and broil until the cheese melts.

✱ To serve, line the roll bottoms with lettuce and cover with the broiled top halves.

Grilled Beefsteak Sandwich with Wilted Onions and Black Bean Spread

5 large onions, sliced into $1/3$-inch-thick rings

1 tablespoon olive oil

2 tablespoons vinegar, preferably cider

1 teaspoon sugar

$1/2$ teaspoon salt

1 teaspoon curry powder (or 1 teaspoon cumin plus 1 teaspoon chili powder)

2 tablespoons chopped parsley

Black Bean Spread

1 (19-ounce) can black beans, rinsed and drained

1 tablespoon mayonnaise

2 tablespoons vinegar (any kind)

2 to 3 scallions, green parts only

15 to 20 fresh cilantro leaves

$1/2$ teaspoon garlic powder

$1/4$ teaspoon salt

6 (4-ounce) filets of beef tenderloin, NY strip, or sirloin steak, all visible fat removed

Olive oil

Salt and freshly ground pepper

6 English muffins, split and toasted

12 lettuce leaves, washed and well dried, for garnish (optional)

3 large tomatoes, each cut into 8 slices

SERVES 6

This sandwich can come together quite quickly. While the onions are cooking, grill the steak and prepare the Black Bean Spread.

✳ Place the onions, along with the oil, vinegar, sugar, salt, and curry in a nonstick skillet; cover with a lid and cook over low heat approximately 6 to 8 minutes, or until cooked but still firm to the bite. Remove from the heat and toss with the parsley. Set aside.

✳ While the onions are cooking, prepare the Black Bean Spread. Place all the spread ingredients in a food processor and blend until smooth and creamy. Set aside. (The spread may be covered and stored in the refrigerator for up to 1 week.)

✳ Prepare a grill or preheat the broiler. Lightly brush the beef with oil, sprinkle with salt and pepper, and grill or broil to the desired doneness, approximately 2 to 3 minutes each side for rare to medium rare. Slice across the grain on a slight diagonal.

✳ To assemble the sandwiches, toast the English muffin halves, then slather some of the Black Bean Spread on both sides. Top each sandwich with some lettuce leaves, tomato slices, sliced beef, and wilted onions.

Spicy Grilled Beef Salad

SERVES 6

This makes a delicious warm salad when tossed with the heated vinaigrette; it can also be served at room temperature with a chilled dressing.

Spice Mix

1/2 teaspoon ground cumin

1/2 teaspoon curry powder

1/2 teaspoon garlic powder

1/8 teaspoon cayenne pepper

Dressing

1 cup chicken stock (homemade or low-sodium canned)

1 tablespoon cornstarch

1/4 cup peanut oil

1/4 cup cider vinegar, or wine vinegar

1/2 teaspoon sugar

1/2 teaspoon salt

1/4 teaspoon coarsely ground fresh pepper

1 1/2 pounds lean beef such as flank steak, beef tenderloin, or sirloin

Olive oil

Salt and freshly ground pepper

Salad

6 large handfuls mixed greens, such as radicchio, Belgian endive, and Boston Bibb, washed and well dried

12 scallions, white parts only, cut into 3-inch pieces

6 tomatoes, sliced horizontally 1/4 inch thick

1/4 cup roasted peanuts, toasted, for garnish (optional)

2 tablespoons chopped parsley, for garnish (optional)

✳ Preheat the oven to 325° F. Combine the cumin, curry, garlic, and cayenne in small ovenproof sauté pan and toast in the oven for approximately 5 minutes until the spices release their aroma. (Alternatively, you can toast the spices on the stove top over low heat, taking care not to let them burn.) Set aside.

✳ To make the dressing, in small sauce pot, combine the chicken stock and cornstarch. Bring the mixture to a boil over medium-high heat. Lower the heat and simmer, whisking continuously, until the mixture thickens, approximately 1 to 2 minutes. Remove from the heat.

✳ In a medium bowl, whisk together the thickened stock, half of the toasted spice mix, the oil, vinegar, sugar, salt, and pepper. Set in the refrigerator if planning on serving a chilled salad, or leave hot for a warm salad.

✱ Rub the beef all over with the remaining half of the spice mix. Prepare a grill or preheat the broiler. Lightly brush the beef with oil, sprinkle with salt and pepper, and grill or broil to the desired doneness, approximately 2 to 3 minutes each side for rare to medium rare. Slice across the grain on a slight diagonal.

✱ To serve, place the greens in a mixing bowl and toss with just enough of the dressing to lightly coat the leaves. In a separate bowl, toss the the scallions and tomatoes with just enough dressing to coat. (Reserve and refrigerate any leftover dressing for another salad.)

✱ Divide the greens evenly among 6 plates and top with the scallions and a few tomato slices. Arrange the beef slices on top of the tomatoes and sprinkle the peanuts and chopped parsley all over, if desired, to garnish.

Gourmet Vegetable Turnovers

2 garlic cloves, minced, plus ¼ teaspoon oil, or 1 teaspoon prepared minced garlic (see page 17)

1 tablespoon olive oil

1 medium (½ cup) onion, cut into small dice

½ large leek, white part only, halved lengthwise and sliced on the diagonal into ¼-inch pieces (1 cup)

1 medium red pepper, cut into matchsticks

1 (15-ounce) can butter beans (or white kidney or cannellini), rinsed and drained

1 (14-ounce) can artichoke hearts, rinsed, drained, and quartered

¼ teaspoon freshly ground pepper

3 ounces oil-cured olives, pitted and coarsely chopped

6 ounces goat cheese

1 box (2 sheets) puff pastry dough

1 egg, beaten

MAKES 6 TURNOVERS

This is a wonderful first course for a dinner party. You can make the vegetables ahead and use store-bought puff pastry. When your guests arrive, slip the turnovers into the oven and they'll be ready just in time for dinner.

✳ In a large skillet, sauté garlic over medium heat in oil until golden, approximately 1 to 2 minutes. Add the onion and continue sautéing until translucent, approximately 3 to 4 minutes. Add the leek and pepper and sauté for an additional 3 minutes, or until the vegetables are softened but not mushy.

✳ Remove the pan from the heat. Add the beans, artichokes, and pepper and gently mix together. Turn the vegetable mixture out onto a baking sheet to cool. When cooled, transfer the vegetables to a large bowl and mix together with the olives and cheese.

✳ Preheat the oven to 400° F. Lightly grease a baking sheet.

✳ To assemble the turnovers, cover a large cutting board with plastic wrap, tucking the ends under the edges of the board. Cut each rectangular sheet of pastry in half, widthwise. Rewrap one of the halves for another use. Using a rolling pin, roll the pastry to less than ⅛-inch thickness. Cut each half vertically into 2 strips. You should have a total of 6 strips.

✳ Brush all the edges of the pastry well with the beaten egg. Evenly divide the filling into 6 portions and mound each portion onto the center of each pastry strip.

✳ Make a 1-inch slice into all four corners of each pastry piece. Fold both long flaps up, then fold the short side flaps, pinching the top corners to make a triangle. Brush the corners with the beaten egg to seal the edges.

✳ Place the filled turnovers on the baking sheet and bake for 25 minutes, or until the turnovers are golden brown. Serve immediately.

Stuffed Mediterranean Pita Sandwiches

SERVES 6

If you want to serve these sandwiches as finger food, use hearty bread cut into squares and top with the vegetable mixture.

2 cloves garlic, minced, plus ¼ teaspoon oil, or 1 teaspoon prepared minced garlic (see page 17)

6 large portobello mushrooms, stems removed and caps cut into ½-inch-thick slices

1 ½ onions, thinly sliced (approximately 1 ½ cups)

1 large head (approximately 1 pound) escarole, washed, well dried, and coarsely chopped

2 bunches (approximately 1 pound) arugula, washed, well dried, and coarsely chopped

25 basil leaves (approximately 1 cup)

1 (15-ounce) can chickpeas, rinsed and drained

Salt and freshly ground pepper

6 ounces feta cheese, preferably seasoned with herbs, crumbled

6 sandwich-size pita rounds, preferably whole wheat, cut in half

3 plum tomatoes, cut ¼ inch thick (approximately 6 slices each), for garnish (optional)

✱ In large nonstick skillet, sauté the garlic over low heat, approximately 1 to 2 minutes, or until aromatic. Add the mushrooms, cover the pan, and cook for approximately 3 minutes, or until soft.

✱ Remove the mushrooms and garlic from the pan and set aside. Add the onions to the pan along with 2 tablespoons of water, cover, and steam for 2 to 3 minutes, or until translucent. Add the greens, basil, and chickpeas to the pan, cover, and continue steaming only until greens wilt, 1 to 2 minutes. Remove from the heat and toss with half of the cheese and the mushrooms. Season with salt and pepper to taste.

✱ To assemble the sandwiches, stuff each pita half with the mushroom and greens mixture and slices of tomatoes, if desired. Garnish with the remaining cheese.

Meals in a Muffin

3 eggs
$1/4$ cup oil
$1/4$ cup brown sugar
3 cups all-purpose flour
1 teaspoon salt
1 $1/2$ teaspoons baking soda
2 cups buttermilk
1 teaspoon chopped fresh parsley
1 teaspoon chopped fresh chives

Boursin and Herb Filling

6 ounces Boursin cheese with garlic
$3/4$ cup chopped scallions,
   green parts only
$3/4$ cup chopped parsley

Tomato, Mozzarella, and Pepperoni

$3/4$ cup tomato sauce
3 ounces mozzarella cheese
3 ounces pepperoni

**MAKES 6
GIANT MUFFINS**

These oversized muffins, stuffed with savory fillings, are perfect for a packed lunch or a midday snack. Adults will appreciate the Boursin and Herb Filling while kids will love the traditional flavors of pizza. You can vary the filling according to your taste.

✷ In an electric mixer or using a hand mixer, beat the eggs, oil, and brown sugar together on low speed.

✷ In a separate bowl, mix together the flour, salt, and baking soda. Add the mixed dry ingredients alternately with the buttermilk and herbs to the egg mixture, and blend just until incorporated. (Do not overmix or it will toughen the batter.)

✷ Mix together the preferred filling ingredients.

✷ Preheat the oven to 375° F. Lightly grease a nonstick giant-size muffin tin (3 $1/2$- x 1 $3/4$-inch) and fill each with $1/4$ cup of batter. (If you don't have a giant tin, the batter should fill 12 regular-size muffin tins.) Divide the preferred filling evenly among the muffin cups, approximately 3 ounces per muffin, then top each with an additional $1/4$ cup batter.

✷ Bake for 35 minutes, until the tops are golden brown and a toothpick inserted into the center comes out clean.

Grilled Potatoes with Aioli

Aioli

2 egg yolks

2 to 4 cloves garlic, chopped

2 tablespoons seasoned rice wine vinegar

1 1/2 cups peanut oil

Salt and freshly ground pepper

6 to 8 new potatoes

1/4 cup roasted garlic-flavored olive oil,
  or good quality olive oil

SERVES 4

Grilling expert
Ted Reader provides
this surefire recipe
for perfect potatoes.
Because the potatoes
are only on the grill
for a few minutes,
he recommends cook-
ing them with the lid
on to enhance their
smoky flavor.

✳ To make the aioli, in a food processor or blender, combine the egg yolks, garlic, and vinegar. Pulse on and off a few times until blended. With the motor running, gradually add the oil in a slow, steady stream and continue processing until thick. Add the salt and pepper to taste. Store in the refrigerator until serving time.

✳ Pierce the potatoes in several places. Place in the microwave, arranging 1 inch apart in a circle. Microwave on High until the potatoes just start to soften, approximately 5 to 7 minutes. Do not overcook; the potatoes should be quite firm. Alternatively, bring a pot of water to a boil and cook the potatoes just until they begin to soften, but are not fully cooked.

✳ Cut the potatoes into chunks and place in a single layer in a grill basket(s). You may need to do this in two batches. Place the potatoes on the grill over high heat, cover with the barbecue lid, and grill, turning every 2 minutes, until the potatoes are crisp and golden brown, approximately 10 to 12 minutes in total. If cooking the potatoes in batches, wrap the grilled potatoes loosely in foil (do not seal) and place in warm oven or at edge of grill while preparing the remaining potatoes.

✳ Serve the potatoes while still warm, along with the aioli.

Mashed Potatoes with Escarole, Bacon, and Roasted Garlic

SERVES 6

You will only need half of the roasted garlic for this recipe but it is easier to roast an entire head and save the extra garlic for another use. If you plan on serving these potatoes with the meatloaf (page 84), roast the garlic at the same time the meatloaf is baking.

1 head garlic

1 1/2 pounds (approximately 5 medium) Yukon Gold or Russet potatoes, peeled and cut into 1/2-inch dice

2 ounces (approximately 3 strips) bacon, cut into small dice

1 small head (approximately 4 cups) escarole or other dark green leaf, washed, dried, and cut into 2-inch pieces

1/4 teaspoon freshly ground pepper

1 1/4 cup low-fat milk, warmed

1/2 teaspoon salt

✳ Preheat the oven to 350° F. Slice just enough of the top of the garlic head so that the tips are exposed, then tightly wrap in foil, and roast for 40 minutes, or until golden brown and extremely soft. Squeeze the bulbs to remove the roasted cloves.

✳ In a large pot, place the potatoes and enough cold, salted water to cover the potatoes by 2 inches and bring to a boil; cook over medium heat for approximately 20 minutes, or until tender when pierced with a fork. Drain and set aside.

✳ In a large sauté pan, cook the bacon over medium-high heat until crisp, approximately 8 to 10 minutes. Remove the bacon and set aside. (For a lower fat version, remove the pan fat.) Either way, add the escarole and pepper to the pan, cover, and cook for 2 minutes, or just until wilted.

✳ In an electric mixer, mash the potatoes with the warm milk, half the roasted garlic, and salt. Fold in the escarole and crumble in the bacon. Serve immediately.

Grilled Mixed Vegetables with Dijon Vinaigrette

8 to 10 large white mushrooms
8 to 10 shiitake mushrooms
1 small zucchini
1 small eggplant
1 red bell pepper
1 yellow bell pepper
1 red onion
10 to 12 thin asparagus spears
12 cloves garlic

Dijon Vinaigrette
$1/3$ cup balsamic vinegar
1 tablespoon Dijon mustard
2 cloves garlic, minced
2 to 3 tablespoons chopped fresh
  coriander
$3/4$ cup extra-virgin olive oil

SERVES 4 TO 8

This recipe was developed by Canadian chef, Ted Reader, who suggests that you vary the vegetable assortment according to your taste and the season. For a more pronounced flavor, marinate the vegetables overnight.

✳ Prepare the vegetables for grilling: Slice the mushrooms into halves or quarters, depending on the size. Cut the zucchini and eggplant in half lengthwise, then into $1/2$-inch slices. Cut the peppers in half, remove the seeds, and then cut into thin strips.

✳ Slice the tops of the onions and peel, keeping the ends on. Slice the onion in half vertically through the root. Cut each half into quarters, making sure not to cut through the root so that the wedges hold together.

✳ Trim the coarse ends of asparagus, then blanch in boiling water for 30 seconds; drain and then cool under running water to stop the cooking. Replenish the pot with clean, salted water and boil the garlic for 4 minutes. Drain.

✳ Prepare a grill. Place the vegetables in a grill basket and grill over medium-high heat, turning periodically, for 15 to 20 minutes, or until the vegetables are tender and slightly charred.

✳ Meanwhile, prepare the vinaigrette: In a small bowl, mix together the vinegar, mustard, garlic, and coriander. Gradually whisk in the olive oil until thickened.

✳ Transfer the vegetables to a large bowl and add enough vinaigrette to coat. (Refrigerate any leftover vinaigrette for another use.) Toss lightly and serve at room temperature.

Acorn Squash with Maple Syrup

1 large acorn squash, cut in half, seeds
   removed, and cut into 6 wedges
1/4 cup maple syrup
1/4 cup dark rum

1/2 teaspoon cinnamon
2 tablespoons unsalted butter, melted
Pinch of salt

SERVES 6

This simple accompaniment is home cooking at its best.

✴ Preheat the oven to 375° F. Lightly grease an ovenproof casserole dish. Place the acorn wedges, cut-side down, in the casserole.

✴ In a small bowl, mix the maple syrup, rum, and cinnamon together. Pour the mixture evenly over the squash.

✴ Bake the squash for 45 minutes. (After 30 minutes, flip the squash over and continue baking.) Add the butter and the salt to the pan and continue baking for an additional 30 minutes, basting the squash with the maple syrup mixture every 10 minutes to prevent it from drying out, until the squash can be easily pierced with a fork. Serve immediately.

Glazed Carrots with Grapes and Walnuts

1 large bunch carrots, peeled and sliced
   1/4 inch thick (approximately 6 cups)
1/4 cup unsalted butter
1 cup chicken stock (homemade or
   low-sodium canned) or water

3 tablespoons sugar
1 cup seedless red grapes,
   cut in half
1/2 cup chopped walnuts
Salt and freshly ground pepper

SERVES 6 TO 8

The carrots and the grapes can be prepared for cooking up to 8 hours in advance. Reprinted from *Casual Occasions Cookbook* (Weldon Owen).

✴ In a wide sauté pan over high heat, combine the carrots, butter, stock or water, and sugar. Bring to a boil, then reduce the heat to medium low. Simmer, uncovered, until the carrots are tender and the pan juices are reduced to a syrupy glaze, approximately 8 to 10 minutes.

✴ Stir in the grapes and walnuts and season to taste with salt and freshly ground pepper. Serve immediately.

PIZZA AND PASTA

Sourdough Pizza with Potatoes and Caramelized Onions

Pizza Dough

1 tablespoon instant active dry yeast

3 cups all-purpose unbleached white flour

1 1/2 teaspoons salt

2 tablespoons Sourdough Bread Enhancement Formula™ (see page 16)

1 cup water, plus 1 to 2 additional tablespoons if needed

Toppings

3 Vidalia onions, already caramelized (see page 21 for instructions)

1 pound Yukon Gold or Russet potatoes, scrubbed

1/4 cup olive oil

Coarse salt and freshly ground pepper

✳ To prepare the dough, place the yeast, flour, salt, Sourdough Bread Enhancement Formula™, and water in a bread machine; program it for Dough or Manual, and press the start button. Add more water if necessary to make a soft, slightly tacky dough. At the end of the final cycle, remove the dough to a lightly floured work surface. The dough will still be quite soft. Knead it by hand for a few minutes, adding only enough flour to make it form a smooth, soft ball. Cover it with a cloth and let it rest on the work surface for 30 minutes. Set aside while you prepare the toppings.

✳ Strain three caramelized onions from the Crock-Pot, cut into thick slices, and set aside.

✳ Place the potatoes in a large pot filled with water and cook for 5 minutes until parboiled. Remove with a slotted spoon and drain well, patting with paper towels. Cut into 1/4-inch-thick slices.

✳ Preheat the oven to 475° F with the rack adjusted in the center position. On a floured surface, stretch or roll out the dough into a 16-inch circle and place it on a perforated or regular pizza pan. Spread with a layer of onions, leaving a 1-inch border around the edge, then top with a layer of potatoes. Drizzle evenly with olive oil and sprinkle with salt and pepper.

✳ Transfer to the preheated oven and bake until the crust is well browned and the potatoes are soft, approximately 20 to 25 minutes. Remove from the oven and place the broiler on high. Broil the pizza for 3 to 4 minutes, or until the potatoes are golden brown and crisp. Serve hot or at room temperature.

SERVES 8 TO 10

This recipe, by Lora Brody, demonstrates the wonder of modern technology. You'll need a bread machine to make the pizza dough and a Crock-Pot to caramelize the onions. The onions must be made a day in advance. The dough can also be used to make bread sticks as well as rolls, loaves, and focaccia. Leave the peel on the potatoes—it is a great source of iron. Reprinted from *Pizza, Focaccia, Filled & Flat Breads from your Bread Machine* (William Morrow & Co.).

Basic Pizza Dough

**MAKES 2 (12-INCH)
ROUND PIZZAS**

This versatile dough comes from James McNair's seminal book on pizza. It can be used for any type of pizza: traditional or contemporary, flat or deep-dish, topped, stuffed, or folded. The recipe can also be doubled and frozen for future pizzas. Reprinted from *Pizza* (Chronicle Books).

1 tablespoon sugar
1 cup warm water (110 to 115° F)
1 envelope (¹/₄ ounce) active dry yeast

3 ¹/₄ cups unbleached all-purpose flour
1 teaspoon salt
¹/₄ cup olive oil, preferably extra-virgin

✳ In a small bowl, dissolve the sugar in the warm water. Sprinkle the yeast over the water and stir gently until it dissolves, approximately 1 minute. Let stand in a warm spot until a thin layer of foam covers the surface, approximately 5 minutes.

✳ **To mix and knead the dough by hand,** combine 3 cups of the flour with the salt in a large mixing bowl. Make a well in the center of the flour and pour in the yeast mixture and the oil, if desired. Using a wooden spoon, vigorously stir the flour into the well, beginning in the center and working toward the sides of the bowl, until the flour is incorporated and the soft dough just begins to hold together. Turn the dough out onto a lightly floured surface. Dust your hands with flour and knead the dough gently for 5 minutes, gradually adding just enough of the remaining flour until the dough is no longer sticky. Continue kneading until the dough is smooth, elastic, and shiny, 10 to 15 minutes longer. Knead the dough only until it feels smooth and springy.

✳ **To mix and knead the dough in a food processor,** add 3 cups of the flour and the salt to the work bowl fitted with the metal blade or a dough hook. Pulse for approximately 5 seconds to combine the ingredients. Add the yeast mixture and oil, if desired, and process continuously until the dough forms a single ball, approximately 30 seconds. If the dough is sticky, continue processing while gradually adding just enough of the remaining flour for the dough to lose its stickiness. If the dough is dry and crumbly, gradually add warm water until it is smooth. Turn the dough out onto a lightly floured surface and knead by hand as described above for 2 minutes.

✳ After mixing and kneading the dough, shape the dough, and place it in a well-oiled bowl, turning to coat completely on all sides with oil. Cover the bowl tightly with plastic wrap and set to rise in a warm place until doubled in bulk, approximately 1 to 1½ hours.

✳ Punch down the dough as soon as it has doubled in bulk. Shape it into a ball, pressing out all the air bubbles. To shape a flat pizza, place the ball of dough on a lightly floured surface and dust the top lightly with flour. Using the heels of your hands, press the dough into a circle or other desired shape, then roll it out with a lightly floured rolling pin until it is ¹/₄ inch thick, keeping the edges a little thicker than the center. While rolling, pick up the dough and turn it over several times to stretch it. Rest one hand near the edge of the dough and use the other hand to push the dough against it to form a slight rim around the perimeter of the dough. Fill and bake as quickly as possible.

Salad Pizza

Basic Pizza Dough (see page 50) or
  approximately 2 pounds
  purchased dough
Vegetable oil for brushing, if using
  a pizza screen or pizza pan
Cornmeal for dusting, if using
  a pizza peel
Olive oil, preferably extra-virgin
1 tablespoon minced or pressed garlic
3 cups freshly shredded mozzarella
  (approximately 12 ounces)
1 cup freshly grated Parmesan cheese,
  preferably Parmigiano-Reggiano
  (approximately 4 ounces)

Balsamic Vinaigrette

2 tablespoons balsamic vinegar
1 teaspoon Dijon-style mustard
$1/2$ teaspoon sugar
$1/4$ teaspoon salt, or to taste
$1/4$ teaspoon freshly ground pepper
$1/4$ cup olive oil, preferably extra-virgin

4 cups small whole or torn tender salad
  greens, rinsed, dried, and chilled
$1/2$ small red onion, cut in half, then thinly
  sliced and separated into half rings
Pesticide-free edible flower petals such as
  nasturtium or calendulas (optional)

**SERVES 4 TO 6
AS A MAIN COURSE;
8 TO 10 AS AN
APPETIZER**

The concept behind
this James McNair
creation is to top
a hot cheese pizza
with a refreshing
mound of cool, crisp
salad. The pie is then
folded over and eaten
as a sandwich. For
variety, substitute
your favorite cheese
and salad dressing.
Reprinted from
*James McNair's
Vegetarian Pizza*
(Chronicle Books).

✳ Prepare the Basic Pizza Dough (see page 50) and set it aside to rise. If using purchased dough, set aside.

✳ Preheat the oven to 500° F. Brush a pizza screen or ventilated pizza pan with vegetable oil or dust a pizza peel with cornmeal; set aside. Shape the pizza dough as directed in the basic recipe.

✳ Brush each dough round all over with olive oil, then sprinkle with the garlic and top with the mozzarella cheese, leaving a ½-inch border around the edges. Sprinkle with the Parmesan cheese and drizzle evenly with olive oil.

✳ Transfer the pies to the preheated oven and bake until the crusts are crisp and the cheese is bubbly, approximately 10 to 15 minutes.

✳ Meanwhile, to make the vinaigrette, in a bowl or in a jar with a cover combine the vinegar, mustard, sugar, and salt and pepper to taste. Whisk well or cover and shake to blend well. Add the olive oil and whisk or shake until emulsified. Alternatively, the ingredients may be mixed in a food processor or blender.

✳ Just before the pizza is done, combine the salad greens, onion, and flower petals, if desired, in a bowl. Pour on the vinaigrette to taste and toss well.

✳ Remove the pizzas from the oven to a cutting tray or board and lightly brush the edges of the crusts with olive oil. Mound the salad on the pizzas and serve immediately. At the table, slice each pizza in half. Instruct diners to fold each half together around the salad and eat out of hand like a sandwich.

Mozzarella and Tomato Pizza

**SERVES 4 TO 6
AS A MAIN COURSE;
8 TO 10 AS AN
APPETIZER**

This recipe is James McNair's version of the classic Pizza Margherita, originally created in honor of Italy's nineteenth-century Queen Margherita. It essential that you use the finest ingredients—fresh cheese, vine-ripened tomatoes, and high-quality olive oil. Reprinted from *Pizza* (Chronicle Books).

Basic Pizza Dough (see page 50), or approximately 2 pounds purchased dough

Cornmeal, for dusting, if using a pizza peel

Approximately 1/2 cup olive oil, preferably extra-virgin

2 1/2 cups (approximately 10 ounces) shredded fresh mozzarella cheese, preferably imported, made in part from water buffalo's milk

4 cups peeled, seeded, chopped, and well-drained vine-ripened Italian plum tomatoes (approximately 2 pounds), or 1 1/2 (28-ounce) cans Italian plum tomatoes, well drained, seeded, and chopped

1 tablespoon minced fresh oregano, or 1 teaspoon dried oregano

Salt

1/2 cup (approximately 2 ounces) freshly grated Parmesan cheese, preferably Parmigiano-Reggiano

1/2 cup shredded fresh basil (optional)

✻ Prepare the basic pizza dough (see page 50), and set it aside to rise. If using purchased dough, set aside.

✻ Preheat the oven to 500° F. Brush a pizza screen or ventilated pizza pan with vegetable oil or dust a pizza peel with cornmeal; set aside. Shape the pizza dough as directed in the basic recipe.

✻ Brush the dough all over with olive oil, then evenly cover with the mozzarella cheese, leaving a 1/2-inch border around the edges. Cover the cheese with the tomatoes, then sprinkle with the oregano, salt to taste, and about half of the Parmesan cheese. Drizzle evenly with olive oil.

✻ Transfer the pizza to the preheated oven and bake until the crust is golden brown and puffy, approximately 10 minutes. Remove from the oven to a cutting tray or board and lightly brush the edges of the crust with olive oil. Sprinkle with the remaining Parmesan cheese and the shredded basil, if desired. Slice and serve immediately.

Olive Paste Pizza

Basic Pizza Dough (see page 50), or approximately 2 pounds purchased dough, or 2 large or 4 to 6 individual-sized prebaked crusts

1 cup pitted imported ripe olives, such as Niçoise

1/2 cup firmly packed fresh basil leaves

3 tablespoons capers, rinsed and drained

2 tablespoons coarsely chopped garlic

1/4 cup olive oil, preferably extra-virgin

Approximately 2 tablespoons freshly squeezed lemon juice

Salt

1/2 teaspoon freshly ground pepper

Vegetable oil for brushing, if using a pizza screen or pizza pan

Cornmeal for dusting, if using a pizza peel

Olive oil, preferably extra-virgin, for brushing crust and drizzling on top

4 cups freshly shredded semisoft cheese such as Morbier, Port-du-Salut, or Taleggio (approximately 20 ounces)

2 cups (approximately 1 pound) chopped, peeled, and well-drained ripe tomato

1 cup sliced (approximately 1 medium) red onion, separated into half rings

Shredded fresh basil, for garnish

Finely diced fresh red or yellow bell peppers, for garnish

**SERVES 4 TO 6
AS A MAIN COURSE;
8 TO 10 AS AN
APPETIZER**

James McNair created this intensely flavored vegetarian pizza by omitting the anchovies traditionally found in the Provençal olive paste known as tapenade. Reprinted from *James McNair's Vegetarian Pizza* (Chronicle Books).

✳ Prepare the Basic Pizza Dough (see page 50) and set it aside to rise. If using purchased dough or prebaked crusts, set aside.

✳ Preheat the oven to 500° F. In a food processor fitted with the metal blade or in a blender, combine the olives, basil leaves, capers, garlic, and the 1/4 cup olive oil. Purée until smooth. Season to taste with lemon juice, salt, and pepper and blend well. Set aside.

✳ Brush a pizza screen or ventilated pizza pan with vegetable oil or dust a pizza peel with cornmeal; set aside. Shape the pizza dough as directed in the basic recipe.

✳ Brush the raw dough or the prebaked crusts all over with olive oil or other vegetable oil, then spread with the olive paste, leaving a 1/2-inch border around the edges. Distribute the cheese over the olive paste, top with the tomato and onion, and drizzle evenly with olive oil.

✳ Transfer the pie to the preheated oven and bake until the crust is crisp and the cheese is bubbly, approximately 8 minutes for prebaked crusts, or 10 to 15 minutes for fresh dough. Remove from the oven to a cutting tray or board and lightly brush the edges of the crust with olive oil. Sprinkle with the shredded basil and diced peppers. Slice and serve immediately.

Pizza with Garlic-Glazed Chicken

**SERVES 4 TO 6
AS A MAIN COURSE;
8 TO 10 AS AN
APPETIZER**

Don't be alarmed
by the huge quantity
of garlic called for in
this recipe by James
McNair. The aromatic
bulb turns sweet
and succulent during
the cooking.
Reprinted from *Pizza*
(Chronicle Books).

Basic Pizza Dough (see page 50), or
    approximately 2 pounds purchased
    dough
1/4 cup sesame seeds
2 heads garlic, broken into cloves,
    peeled and coarsely chopped
2 teaspoons crushed dried red
    chili pepper
1/2 cup soy sauce
5 tablespoons honey

1 1/2 cups rice vinegar
Approximately 3/4 cup vegetable oil
5 boneless and skinless chicken breast
    halves, cut into bite-sized pieces
Cornmeal for dusting, if using a pizza peel
2 cups (approximately 8 ounces) grated
    Gruyère cheese
1 cup (approximately 4 ounces) shredded
    mozzarella cheese
1/4 cup chopped green onions

✱ Prepare the Basic Pizza Dough (see page 50) and set it aside to rise. If using purchased dough, set aside.

✱ Preheat the oven to 500° F. Place the sesame seeds in a small skillet and toast over medium heat, stirring or shaking the pan, until golden, approximately 4 minutes. Empty onto a plate to cool.

✱ Combine the garlic, crushed red pepper, soy sauce, honey, and vinegar in a bowl.

✱ Heat 1/4 cup of the vegetable oil in a sauté pan or a large skillet over medium-high heat and sauté the chicken until opaque on all sides, approximately 3 minutes. Remove with a slotted spoon and reserve. Pour the garlic mixture into the skillet and cook over medium-high heat, stirring frequently, until the sauce is reduced to the consistency of a syrup, approximately 15 minutes. Return the chicken to the pan and cook, stirring constantly, until the pieces are lightly glazed, approximately 2 minutes. Remove from the heat and reserve.

✱ Brush a pizza screen or ventilated pizza pan with vegetable oil or dust a pizza peel with cornmeal; set aside. Shape the pizza dough as directed in the basic recipe.

✱ Brush the dough all over with vegetable oil, then top with a layer of each of the cheeses and the glazed chicken, leaving a 1/2-inch border around the edges. Sprinkle with the remaining cheese and the green onion and drizzle evenly with olive oil.

✱ Transfer the pie to the preheated oven and bake until the crust is crisp and the cheese is bubbly, approximately 10 to 15 minutes. Remove from the oven to a cutting tray or board and lightly brush the edges of the crust with vegetable oil. Sprinkle with the toasted sesame seeds, slice, and serve immediately.

Banana Satay Pizza

Basic Pizza Dough (see page 50), or
   approximately 2 pounds purchased
   dough

Peanut Sauce

2/3 cup smooth peanut butter

1 1/2 cups homemade or sweetened
   canned coconut milk

1/4 cup vegetable stock, preferably
   homemade

1/4 cup heavy cream

1/4 cup freshly squeezed lemon juice

2 tablespoons soy sauce

2 tablespoons brown sugar or molasses

1 teaspoon grated fresh ginger

2 teaspoons minced or pressed garlic

Ground cayenne pepper

Vegetable oil for brushing, if using
   a pizza screen or pizza pan

Cornmeal for dusting, if using a pizza peel

Canola oil or other high-quality
   vegetable oil

6 ripe, yet firm bananas

3 tablespoons unsalted butter, melted,
   or more as needed

Chopped roasted peanuts, for garnish

Grated lime zest, for garnish

**SERVES 4 TO 6
AS A MAIN COURSE;
8 TO 10 AS AN
APPETIZER**

This dessert pizza,
created by James
McNair, pairs the
sweet creaminess of
bananas with a spicy
Southeast Asian
peanut sauce.
Reprinted from
*James McNair's
Vegetarian Pizza*
(Chronicle Books).

✱ Prepare the Basic Pizza Dough (see page 50) and set it aside to rise. If using purchased dough, set aside.

✱ Preheat the oven to 500° F. To make the peanut sauce, in a saucepan combine the peanut butter, coconut milk, stock, cream, lemon juice, soy sauce, brown sugar or molasses, ginger, garlic, and cayenne pepper to taste. Place over medium heat and cook, stirring constantly, until the sauce is as thick as a cheese sauce, approximately 15 minutes. Reserve. (This mixture can also be made up to 24 hours ahead, covered, and refrigerated. Return to room temperature before using.)

✱ Brush a pizza screen or ventilated pizza pan with vegetable oil or dust a pizza peel with cornmeal; set aside. Shape the pizza dough as directed in the basic recipe.

✱ Brush the dough all over with the canola oil or other vegetable oil, then top with the peanut sauce, leaving a ½-inch border around the edges. Slice the bananas lengthwise or into rounds and distribute them over the sauce. Brush the banana slices with the melted butter.

✱ Transfer the pie to the preheated oven and bake until the crust is crisp, 10 to 15 minutes. Remove from the oven to a cutting tray or board and lightly brush the edges of the crust with canola oil or other vegetable oil. Sprinkle with the peanuts and lime zest. Slice and serve immediately.

Bowtie Pasta with Lemon, Capers, Artichokes, and Olives

1 1/2 pounds bowtie pasta (also called *farfalle*)

2 cloves garlic, minced, plus 1/4 teaspoon oil, or 1 teaspoon prepared minced garlic (see page 17)

2 tablespoons cornstarch

4 tablespoons water

3 cups chicken stock (homemade or low-sodium canned)

1/2 cup green Italian cured olives

1/2 cup black Greek Kalamata or Niçoise olives

1 (14-ounce) can artichoke hearts, rinsed, drained, and quartered (or 6 ounces sugar or snap peas)

1/4 cup capers, finely chopped

Zest and juice of 1 lemon

1/2 cup pimentos, cut into thin strips

1/4 cup chopped scallions, green parts only, for garnish

✳ Bring a pot of boiling water to a boil and cook the pasta according to the manufacturer's directions until al dente.

✳ Meanwhile, in a medium saucepan, sauté the garlic in olive oil over medium heat until slightly golden, 1 to 2 minutes. In small bowl, mix the cornstarch with the water. Add to the chicken stock, then add the thickened chicken stock to the pan and bring to a boil.

✳ Drain the pasta and place in a large mixing bowl. Add the thickened chicken stock, the olives, artichokes, capers, and lemon zest and toss well.

✳ To serve, evenly divide the pasta into 6 serving bowls and garnish each serving with the pimentos and scallions.

SERVES 6

This quick, colorful, and easy pasta dish is a wonderful first course for a dinner party. You can use a vegetable stock to make it an all-vegetarian meal. Use half the amount of olives if you are concerned about too much sodium.

Ditalini and Lentil Salad with Smoked Salmon and Escarole

SERVES 6

Ditalini, are tiny, short macaroni. If you can't find it, use another miniature pasta, such as orzo. This dish makes a beautiful presentation when served with smoked salmon.

2 cloves garlic, minced, plus $1/4$ teaspoon oil, or 1 teaspoon prepared minced garlic (see page 17)

$1/2$ tablespoon olive oil

2 carrots, cut into small dice

$1/2$ pound dried lentils

3 cups cool water

2 springs fresh thyme

1 bay leaf

$1/2$ cup (3 ounces) *ditalini*

1 tablespoon olive oil

$1/4$ cup red wine or sherry vinegar

3 plum tomatoes, diced (approximately $1/2$ cup)

$1/3$ bunch scallions, green parts only, chopped, (approximately $1/2$ cup)

1 head escarole, Bibb lettuce, or Belgian endive, washed and dried

12 ounces smoked salmon, thinly sliced (approximately 18 slices)

✱ In medium-sized pot, sauté the garlic in olive oil over medium heat for 1 to 2 minutes until golden. Add the carrots and cook for 2 to 3 minutes until they color slightly. Add the lentils, water, thyme, and bay leaf, and raise the heat to high. When the mixture comes to a boil, cover, reduce the heat, and gently simmer for approximately 25 minutes, or until the lentils are tender and most of the liquid has evaporated. (If the liquid evaporates before the lentils are tender, add additional liquid. Conversely, if they become tender but the mixture is still runny, drain the lentils.)

✱ In the meantime, while the lentils are simmering, cook the *ditalini* in boiling water according to the manufacturer's directions until al dente.

✱ Combine the cooked lentils with the pasta in a bowl and toss with the oil, vinegar, tomatoes, and scallions.

✱ To serve, fan the lettuce leaves on each plate. Evenly distribute the lentils in center of the plates, slightly covering the lettuce leaves. Drape 3 salmon slices over the lentils.

Pasta with Tomato Vinaigrette

Basil Oil

2 1/2 cups tightly packed basil leaves

1 1/2 cup olive oil

Tomato Vinaigrette

8 medium vine-ripened red tomatoes,
    peeled, seeded, and finely chopped

2 tablespoons minced shallots

1 tablespoon minced garlic

6 tablespoons finely chopped fresh
    flat-leaf parsley

1/4 cup fresh lemon juice

1 cup basil oil (see left) or
    extra-virgin olive oil

Salt and freshly ground pepper

1 1/2 pounds dried pasta (such as
    rigatoni or *orecchiette*)

1 cup freshly grated Parmesan or
    pecorino cheese

SERVES 6

Michael Chiarello,
the chef at Tra Vigne
in Napa Valley
who created this dish,
insists that the shape
of pasta you use is
very important.
Small tubes (*rigatoni*)
and "little ears"
(*orecchiette*) both hold
the sauce well. If you
choose a smooth,
straight shape such as
spaghetti, the sauce
will drain into
a pool at the bottom
of the bowl. This
pasta is meant to be
served just slightly
warmer than room
temperature.
Reprinted from
Flavored Oils
(Chronicle Books).

✱ To make your own basil oil, bring a large saucepan of water to a boil. Add the basil and make sure to push the leaves under the boiling water. Blanch the herbs for 5 seconds. Drain into a strainer and immediately plunge into a bowl of ice water. Drain well and squeeze out all the liquid. Purée in a blender with olive oil. Strain the purée immediately through a fine-mesh strainer such as a china cap. Strain again through 4 layers of cheesecloth and put in a sterilized glass bottle. Cover tightly and refrigerate for up to 1 week. Makes approximately 1 cup oil.

✱ To make the tomato vinaigrette, in a large nonaluminum bowl, mix together the tomatoes, shallots, garlic, 1/4 cup of the parsley, lemon juice, and basil oil and season with salt and pepper to taste. Set the mixture aside at room temperature for 15 to 20 minutes to let the flavors develop. If making further ahead, do not salt until 15 minutes before serving, otherwise the salt will draw all the water out of the tomatoes.

✱ In the meantime, bring a large pot of salted water to a boil and cook the pasta according to the manufacturer's directions until al dente. Drain well and toss with the tomato vinaigrette. Add 1/2 cup of cheese and mix well.

✱ To serve, evenly divide the pasta into 6 serving bowls and garnish each serving with the remaining cheese and parsley.

Creamy Pasta Ribbons with Asparagus, Corn, and Sun-Dried Tomatoes

Sauce

4 ounces (1/2 package) Neufchâtel
    cream cheese, at room temperature

1 (15-ounce) can crushed tomatoes

1 garlic clove, minced, plus 1/8 teaspoon
    oil, or 1/2 teaspoon prepared minced
    garlic (see page 17)

1/4 teaspoon salt

1/8 teaspoon coarsely ground fresh pepper

1/2 teaspoon Tabasco sauce

1/2 tablespoon sherry vinegar, or red
    wine, or tarragon vinegar

1 1/2 pounds wide ribboned pasta noodles

15 sun-dried tomato halves (not packed
    in oil)

2 cloves garlic, minced, plus 1/4 teaspoon
    oil, or 1 1/2 teaspoons prepared
    minced garlic (see page 17)

1 tablespoon olive oil

1/2 small onion, thinly sliced
    (approximately 1/2 cup)

1 cup reserved pasta water

8 to 10 stalks asparagus, ends trimmed
    off and cut into 2 1/2-inch pieces

1 (11-ounce) can corn

1/4 teaspoon cayenne pepper

1/4 teaspoon salt

1 tablespoon balsamic vinegar

Parmesan cheese curls, for garnish

2 tablespoons sliced scallions, green
    parts only, for garnish (optional)

SERVES 6

Be sure to reserve
the pasta water after
you cook with it to
add to the sauce. The
water gives moisture
to the vegetables
and body to the sauce
without adding fat.

✳ To make the sauce, place the cream cheese, crushed tomatoes, garlic, salt, pepper, Tabasco, and sherry vinegar into a blender and purée until smooth. Set aside.

✳ Bring a large pot of salted water to a boil and cook the pasta according to the manufacturer's directions until al dente. Reserve the pasta water.

✳ While the pasta is cooking, rehydrate the sun-dried tomatoes by placing them in a bowl with 1/2 cup water, cover, and microwave for approximately 3 minutes. Alternatively, bring a small pot of water to a boil and add the dry tomatoes. Simmer gently for 1 minute, then remove from the heat and set aside for 5 minutes, or until soft. Drain the rehydrated tomatoes and cut each tomato into 3 strips.

✳ In large sauté pan, sauté the garlic in the oil over medium heat until golden, approximately 1 to 2 minutes. Add the onion and sauté for 1 minute, or until translucent. Add 3/4 cup of the reserved pasta water to the pan and then add the asparagus. Cover and steam the asparagus until al dente, approximately 3 to 5 minutes.

✳ Add the rehydrated tomatoes, corn, cayenne, and salt and simmer 1 to 2 minutes until warmed through. Add the drained pasta and vinegar and toss with the sauce, vegetables and the remaining 1/4 cup reserved pasta water.

✳ To serve, evenly divide the pasta into 6 serving bowls and garnish each serving with Parmesan curls and scallions.

Pasta with Creamy Carrot Sauce and Roasted Peppers

1 pound pasta (any kind)

1 tablespoon olive oil

Creamy Carrot Sauce

$^1/_2$ clove garlic, minced, plus $^1/_4$ tea-spoon oil, or $^1/_4$ teaspoon prepared minced garlic (see page 17)

$^1/_2$ tablespoon orange (or apple) juice concentrate, unreconstituted

2 (4-ounce) jars puréed carrot baby food

1 cup reserved pasta water

$^1/_4$ teaspoon salt

$^1/_8$ teaspoon dried dill

$^1/_4$ cup evaporated skim milk

1 teaspoon rice or apple cider vinegar

2 cloves garlic, minced, plus $^1/_4$ teaspoon oil, or 1 teaspoon prepared minced garlic (see page 17)

5 ounces roasted red peppers or pimen-tos (packed in water, not marinated)

1 (14-ounce) can artichoke hearts, drained and quartered

$^1/_8$ teaspoon freshly ground pepper

$^1/_4$ teaspoon dried *fines herbs* mix (optional)

$^1/_2$ cup (3 ounces) oil-cured Moroccan olives, pitted

$^1/_4$ cup dry-roasted, unsalted peanuts (optional)

✱ Bring a large pot of salted water to a boil and cook the pasta according to the manufacturer's instructions until al dente. Strain and reserve the pasta water. Toss the pasta in the olive oil and set aside.

✱ To make the sauce, in a small saucepan, sauté the ½ clove garlic in oil over medium heat until golden, approximately 1 to 2 minutes. Add the orange juice concentrate, puréed carrots, ¼ cup reserved pasta water, salt, and dill and bring to simmer. Remove the saucepan from the heat and stir in the milk and vinegar. Set aside.

✱ In a separate large sauté pan, sauté the 2 cloves garlic in oil over medium heat until lightly golden brown, approximately 1 to 2 minutes. Add remaining ¾ cup reserved pasta water, red peppers, artichokes, ground pepper, and *fines herbs* mix, if desired, and simmer gently to heat thoroughly. Remove the pan from the heat and stir in the olives.

✱ In a large pasta bowl, toss the cooked pasta with the sauce and top with the vegetables. Sprinkle with the peanutes, if desired. Serve immediately.

Risotto with Greens, Gorgonzola, and Walnuts

5 cups chicken stock (homemade or
low-sodium canned)

3 tablespoons olive oil

1/2 large onion, chopped

1 1/2 cups Arborio or medium-grain rice

1/2 cup dry white wine

3 cups thinly sliced greens such as escarole, Swiss chard, or kale

3/4 cup crumbled Gorgonzola cheese

1/2 cup walnuts, toasted and chopped

Salt and freshly ground pepper

✳ In a small saucepan over high heat, bring the chicken stock to a simmer. Reduce the heat to low and keep the liquid hot.

✳ In a heavy medium-sized saucepan over medium-low heat, heat the olive oil and sauté the onion, stirring frequently, until it is translucent, approximately 8 minutes.

✳ To the onion, add the rice and stir until the liquid bubbles and is absorbed slowly. Stir until the liquid is absorbed. Continue cooking, adding the liquid 3/4 cup at a time, and stirring, almost constantly, until the rice starts to soften, approximately 10 minutes.

✳ Add the greens and continue cooking, adding the liquid 1/2 cup at a time, and stirring almost constantly, until the rice is just tender but slightly firm in the center and the mixture is creamy, approximately 10 minutes longer.

✳ Add the Gorgonzola cheese, walnuts, and salt and pepper to taste. Stir to mix well.

✳ To serve, spoon into shallow bowls or onto plates.

SERVES 6

The combination of robust greens, tangy cheese, and toasted nuts makes this an ideal first course. You may substitute Roquefort, Danish blue, or another blue-veined cheese for the Gorgonzola. This recipe was developed by Kristine Kidd, food editor at *Bon Appetit*. Reprinted from *Risotto: Williams-Sonoma Kitchen Library* (Time Life).

Pea, Tarragon, and Goat Cheese Risotto

SERVES 6

Kristine Kidd
developed this con-
temporary version
of the Venetian
specialty known
as *risi e bisi,* a cross
between risotto
and soup. Reprinted
from *Risotto:
Williams-Sonoma
Kitchen Library*
(Time Life).

5 ½ cups chicken stock (homemade or
    low-sodium canned)

3 tablespoons olive oil

½ large onion, chopped

1 ½ cups Arborio or medium-grain rice

½ cup dry white wine

1 ½ cups shelled fresh peas (or
    frozen peas)

2 teaspoons finely chopped fresh tarragon
    or ¾ teaspoon dried tarragon

½ cup crumbled mild goat cheese

Salt and freshly ground pepper

Fresh tarragon sprigs, for garnish

✳ In a small saucepan over high heat, bring the chicken stock to a simmer. Reduce the heat to low and keep the liquid hot.

✳ In a heavy medium-sized saucepan over medium-low heat, heat the olive oil and sauté the onion, stirring frequently, until it is translucent, approximately 8 minutes.

✳ To the onion add the rice and stir until the liquid bubbles and is absorbed slowly. Stir until the liquid is absorbed. Continue cooking, adding the liquid ¾ cup at a time, and stirring, almost constantly, until the rice starts to soften, approximately 10 minutes.

✳ Add the peas and chopped tarragon and continue cooking, adding the liquid ½ cup at a time, and stirring, almost constantly, until the rice is just tender but slightly firm in the center and the mixture is creamy, approximately 10 minutes longer.

✳ Add the goat cheese and stir until the cheese melts. Add the salt and pepper to taste. Stir to mix well.

✳ To serve, spoon into shallow bowls or onto plates. Garnish with the tarrgon sprigs.

MAIN COURSES

Pacific Coast Chicken
with Jicama-Cucumber Slaw

Marinade

2 teaspoons ground cumin

4 cloves garlic, minced, plus $^1/_2$ teaspoon oil, or 2 teaspoon prepared minced garlic (see page 17)

$^1/_4$ teaspoon red pepper flakes

$^1/_2$ teaspoon dried thyme

$^1/_2$ teaspoon dried sage

$^1/_2$ cup pineapple juice

$^1/_2$ cup apricot nectar

$^1/_2$ cup (1 lime) lime juice

2 tablespoons olive or vegetable oil

$^1/_2$ teaspoon freshly ground pepper

1 teaspoon salt

6 (4-ounce) boneless and skinless chicken breast halves

Slaw

$^1/_2$ jicama (approximately 7 ounces) or white turnip, peeled, and cut into matchsticks

1 large cucumber, peeled, seeded, and thinly sliced on the diagonal

6 to 8 radishes, halved and thinly sliced

2 tablespoons chopped scallions, green parts only, for garnish

Freshly cracked pepper

SERVES 6

In this recipe, the marinade acts as a flavor enhancer for the chicken and a dressing for the slaw. For food safety, it's important to divide the marinade into two bowls—one for the chicken and one for the slaw—so that the chicken marinade is not reused. You can marinate the chicken overnight for even more flavor.

✳ Preheat the oven to 325° F. Place the cumin, garlic, red pepper flakes, thyme, and sage in an ovenproof sauté pan, and toast in the oven for 5 to 6 minutes, or until aromatic.

✳ Mix all the marinade ingredients together and divide into 2 separate bowls. Add the chicken to one bowl, turn to coat well, and set in the refrigerator to marinate for at least 20 minutes or overnight. Place the slaw vegetables in the bowl with the other half of the marinade, toss well, and set in the refrigerator for up to 2 hours.

✳ Prepare a grill or preheat the broiler. Shake the excess marinade off the chicken and grill or broil until golden, approximately 3 to 5 minutes each side, or until cooked through.

✳ To serve, mound ¼ cup of the slaw in the center of each plate. Slice each chicken breast on the bias into 3 or 4 medallions and arrange them next to the slaw. Garnish with the scallions and freshly cracked pepper.

Crusty Coconut Chicken with Grilled Pineapple and Chayote

Marinade

3 tablespoons Dijon-style mustard

3 tablespoons apricot preserves

1 tablespoon sesame oil

$1/4$ teaspoon red pepper flakes

$1/4$ teaspoon salt

6 (4-ounce) boneless and skinless
   chicken breast halves

Crust

$1/2$ cup sweetened shredded coconut

1 cup crushed cornflakes

1 whole fresh pineapple, peeled and cut
   into $3/4$-inch-thick slices

2 chayotes, peeled, pitted, and sliced
   into $3/4$-inch-thick wedges

✱ In a large bowl, combine all the marinade ingredients, place the chicken in the bowl, and coat well. Place the bowl in the refrigerator and allow the chicken to marinate for 20 minutes.

✱ In a shallow bowl, mix the coconut and cornflakes together. Remove the chicken from the marinade, shaking off any excess, and roll the chicken into the cornflake mix, coating evenly on all sides. Reserve the marinade.

✱ Preheat the oven to 325° F. Place the chicken on a baking sheet and bake for 20 minutes, or until cooked through. Raise the heat to 400° F and cook for an additional 5 minutes to crisp the crust.

✱ Prepare a grill. In a sauce pot, bring the reserved marinade to a boil and cook for 2 minutes. Brush the fresh pineapple and chayote slices with the cooked marinade. Place directly on the grill and cook until golden in color and softened slightly but not mushy, approximately 3 to 5 minutes on each side.

✱ To serve, slice each chicken breast in half on the bias and arrange the two halves, alternately with slices of grilled pineapple and chayote, on each plate.

Southwestern Chipotle Chicken

Braising Liquid

1/2 cup tequila, vodka, or white wine

2 tablespoons olive oil

1/2 cup fresh cilantro leaves

1 whole canned chipotle chili in adobo
with 2 teaspoons of the sauce, or
1 fresh jalepeño chili plus 1 drop of
Liquid Smoke™

3 cloves garlic

2 large whole plum tomatoes

4 tablespoons red wine or cider vinegar

4 tablespoons dark Karo syrup, honey,
or maple syrup

4 tablespoons apple juice concentrate

1 teaspoon salt

Zest of 1 lime (or lemon)

Flour, for dredging

1 1/2 pounds boneless and skinless
chicken breast or chicken parts cut
into strips

1 tablespoon olive or vegetable oil

1 red onion, cut into large dice

3 large red potatoes, cut into large dice

1/2 pound parsnips, peeled and cut
into 1-inch chunks

Juice of 1 lime (or lemon)

Fresh cilantro leaves, for garnish
(optional)

SERVES 6

Serve this flavorful
stewed dish over
white rice.

✱ Place all the braising liquid ingredients in a food processor fitted with a metal blade and pulse until smooth. Set aside.

✱ Place the flour in a large shallow bowl. Dredge the chicken strips in the flour, shaking off any excess flour. In a large, ovenproof, nonstick skillet over medium-high heat, sauté the chicken in oil for 2 to 3 minutes on each side, or until dark golden brown. Remove from the pan and set aside.

✱ Add the onion to pan, lower to medium heat, and sauté approximately 5 minutes until slightly caramelized, stirring constantly to prevent the onion from sticking on the bottom of the pan.

✱ Preheat the oven to 325° F.

✱ Add the potatoes, parsnips, and the braising liquid to the pan and bring to boil. Place the chicken on top of the vegetables and cover the pan with a tightly fitting lid. Place the pan in the oven and braise for 35 to 40 minutes, or until the vegetables are tender and the chicken is cooked through. After 20 minutes of braising, stir the contents from top to bottom, to ensure even cooking.

✱ To serve, spoon the vegetables from the pan and evenly distribute onto 6 plates. Top with the chicken and some sauce and drizzle some lime juice of the top. Garnish with cilantro leaves, if desired.

Chinese-Style Asparagus Chicken

SERVES 6

For a beautiful
presentation,
remember to slice
the chicken breasts
on the bias and
fan them out on the
plate. If asparagus
in not in season,
try substituting
string beans.

Flour, for dredging
6 (4-ounce) boneless and skinless
   chicken breast halves
2 tablespoons vegetable oil
1/2 cup sliced almonds
3 cloves garlic, minced, plus 1/3 teaspoon
   oil, or 1 1/2 teaspoons prepared
   minced garlic (see page 17)
1/2 tablespoon chopped ginger or
    1/2 teaspoon powdered ginger

4 tablespoons green onions, green parts
   only, chopped
1 1/2 pounds asparagus, trimmed and
   cut into 2-inch pieces
1/2 cup chicken stock (homemade or
   low-sodium canned)
2 tablespoons soy sauce
1/2 teaspoon red pepper flakes or hot
   bean paste (available in Asian markets)
1 tablespoon vinegar, preferably rice wine

✱ Preheat the oven to 350° F. Place the flour in a shallow bowl, dredge the chicken in flour, coating both sides, and shake off any excess. In a large sauté pan over medium-high heat, sauté the chicken in oil until golden, approximately 3 to 4 minutes on each side. Transfer the chicken from pan to a baking sheet and finish cooking in the oven for approximately 10 minutes, or until cooked through. Set aside.

✱ While the oven is still on, place the almonds on a baking sheet and toast for approximately 10 minutes, or until golden and aromatic. Set aside.

✱ Add the garlic, ginger, and 3 tablespoons of scallions to the sauté pan and cook over medium heat for 1 minute, or until they release their aroma. Add the asparagus and ¼ cup of stock, cover, and steam for 2 minutes, or until done but still firm.

✱ Stir in the soy sauce, pepper flakes, vinegar, and remaining stock, bring to boil, and remove the pan from the heat.

✱ To serve, slice each chicken breast on the bias into 3 or 4 medallions and fan them across each plate. Drizzle the sauce on top and garnish with the reserved green scallions and toasted almonds.

Tuscan Chicken with Creamy White Wine Sauce

SERVES 6

Try using a white wine that is not too dry. You can use half-and-half in lieu of the heavy cream, but skim milk will not work. Serve the chicken over rice.

6 (4-ounce) boneless and skinless
chicken breast halves
Salt and freshly ground pepper
Flour, for dredging
2 tablespoons plus 2 teaspoons olive oil
6 cloves garlic, minced, plus 3/4 teaspoon
oil, or 3 teaspoons prepared minced
garlic (see page 17)
2 teaspoons oil
1 onion, cut into small dice

1 teaspoon dried thyme
1/2 cup white wine
12 sun-dried tomatoes (not packed in oil)
1 cup heavy cream
2 tablespoons chopped fresh parsley
3 ounces cooked ham, such as
Canadian bacon or Boar's Head,
cut into thin strips
1 (15-ounce) can artichoke hearts,
rinsed, drained, and quartered

✳ Season the chicken with salt and pepper. Place the flour in a shallow bowl, dredge the chicken in the flour, and shake off any excess.

✳ Preheat the oven to 325° F. In large sauté pan, sauté chicken in 2 tablespoons of the oil over medium-high heat until brown, approximately 3 to 4 minutes. Transfer the chicken from pan to a baking sheet and finish cooking in the oven for approximately 10 minutes, or until cooked through. Set aside.

✳ Add the garlic to the original sauté pan and sauté in 2 teaspoons of oil over low heat for 1 to 2 minutes, or until it becomes aromatic. Add the onion and continue to sauté for 3 to 4 minutes, or until brown. Add the thyme and sauté for an additional 1 minute until it releases its aroma.

✳ Pour in the white wine and deglaze the pan by using a wooden spoon and scraping the bits that have stuck to the pan. Cook over medium heat until the liquid is reduced in volume by half, approximately 2 to 3 minutes.

✳ To rehydrate the sun-dried tomatoes, bring a small pot of water to a boil and add the dry tomatoes. Simmer gently for 1 minute, then remove from the heat and set aside for 5 minutes, or until soft. Drain the rehydrated tomatoes and slice into strips.

✳ Add the cream to the sauce and season with salt and pepper to taste. Gently simmer over low heat for for approximately 5 minutes or until the sauce thickens slightly and coats the back of a spoon. Add the tomatoes, ham, and artichokes to the pan and simmer for 1 to 2 minutes just to warm through.

✳ To serve, slice each chicken breast on the bias into 3 or 4 medallions and fan them across each plate. Arrange the vegetables around the chicken and drizzle the sauce over the vegetables.

Ivy's Cranberry-Orange Turkey Breast

1 fresh or defrosted uncooked turkey
breast, skin on (approximately
3 pounds)
Salt and freshly ground pepper
4 large onions, peeled, cut in half,
and thinly sliced
4 large carrots, peeled and cut into
1/2-inch slices

1 cup dried cranberries
1 cup dried apricots
6 ounces (3/4 cup) partially defrosted
orange juice concentrate
10 to 12 ounces orange marmalade
2 cups chicken broth (or white wine)
2 teaspoons salt
Freshly ground pepper

SERVES 6

Lora Brody, creator
of this one-pot dish,
thinks it's perfect
for the novice cook,
but even experienced
cooks will appreciate
its simplicity and
color. Use your
favorite dried fruits
as substitutes for
the cranberries and
apricots; apricot
preserves can be
used instead of
orange marmalade.
Reprinted from *The
Kitchen Survival Guide*
(William Morrow
& Co.).

✳ Preheat the oven to 325° F.

✳ Rinse the turkey and pat dry. Place the breast in a Dutch oven or roasting pan and sprinkle with salt and pepper. Place the onions, carrots, cranberries, and apricots around the turkey.

✳ In a bowl, combine the orange juice concentrate, marmalade, and broth and mix well. Pour the mixture over the vegetables and fruit in the pan. Add a little water, if necessary, to make sure there are at least 2 inches of liquid in the bottom of the pan. Cover and cook for approximately 2 hours, or until the internal temperature registers 170° F. Let rest for 10 minutes.

✳ To serve, slice with an electric knife. The turkey is very good served with rice or over noodles.

Stewed Chicken with Chipotles and Prunes

SERVES 6

Although there are
numerous steps to
this chicken dish, it is
easy to prepare. Its
creator, Martha Rose
Schulman, combines
chilies, prunes,
roasted tomatoes,
garlic, and cinnamon
to make a flavorful
stew. It can keep in
the refrigerator for
a few days where the
flavors will mature.
The tomato sauce can
be prepared hours
or even a day ahead.
Reprinted from
Mexican Light
(Bantam Books).

2 ½ quarts water

2 to 3 large or 4 small dried chipotle
chilies

¼ cup salt for the chipotles, plus
additional for the stew

1 medium onion, halved

1 (3-pound) chicken, skin removed and
cut up into serving pieces

8 prunes, pitted

4 large cloves garlic—2 minced and
2 unpeeled to be toasted

2 pounds (8 medium or 4 large) tomatoes
or 2 (28-ounce) cans, drained

2 black peppercorns, ground (a pinch)

1 clove, ground (a pinch)

1 tablespoon canola or olive oil

1 3-inch-long cinnamon stick

✱ Bring 2 cups water to a boil in a saucepan and add the chilies and ¼ cup salt. Stir to dissolve the salt, remove from heat, and let the chilies soak for 3 hours or longer. Flip the chilies over from time to time or weight with a plate so they will soak evenly.

✱ Combine 1 onion half, the remaining water, the chicken, and 2 of the prunes in a large pot and bring to a simmer. Skim any foam that rises. Add 1 teaspoon salt and the minced garlic. Simmer for 15 minutes while you prepare the ingredients for the sauce.

✱ To roast the tomatoes and onion: Preheat the broiler. Line a baking sheet with foil and place the fresh whole tomatoes and the other onion half on it. (Do not attempt to roast canned tomatoes.) Place under the broiler, 2 to 3 inches from the heat. Turn after 2 to 3 minutes, when the tomatoes have charred on one side, and repeat on the other side. The onion will take longer. Turn it several times, until charred and soft-ened, approximately 5 to 10 minutes. Remove from the heat and transfer to a bowl. When the tomatoes are cool enough to handle, peel and core. Set aside.

✱ To toast the garlic: Heat a heavy skillet over medium heat and toast the garlic in its skin, turning or shaking the pan often, until it smells toasty and is blackened in several places, approximately 10 minutes. Remove from the heat and peel.

✱ Strain 2 ½ cups of the stock through a cheesecloth-lined strainer into a measuring cup. Keep the chicken in the remaining stock while you cook the sauce.

✻ Place the roasted onion and tomatoes (or drained canned tomatoes) to a blender along with any juices that have accumulated in the bowl. Add the toasted garlic. Drain the chipotles and rinse thoroughly in several changes of water to rid them of the salt. Add to the blender along with the ground pepper and clove and the 2 prunes you simmered with the chicken. Blend until smooth. Strain into a bowl through a medium-mesh strainer.

✻ Heat the oil in a large heavy casserole or large nonstick skillet over medium-high heat and add a bit of the tomato purée. If it sizzles loudly, add the rest (wait a couple if minutes if it doesn't). Stir together for approximately 3 to 5 minutes, until the sauce thickens slightly, and stir in ½ cup of the strained stock and ½ teaspoon salt. Turn the heat to low and simmer, stirring often, for 20 minutes, until the sauce is fragrant and thick. Add the chicken pieces, the remaining prunes, the cinnamon, the remaining 2 cups of strained stock from the chicken, and more salt to taste. (Strain the remaining stock and freeze or use for cooking rice.) Stir together, cover partially, and simmer over medium-low heat for 30 minutes, stirring from time to time, or until the chicken is tender, but cooked through. Taste and adjust the salt.

✻ To serve the chicken, evenly spoon the chicken and and some sauce over rice, if desired.

Rice-Encrusted Chicken with Pears and Blue Cheese

Crust

Flour, for dredging

1 egg plus 2 egg whites, beaten

1 1/2 cups cooked storebought wild rice mix (see sidebar)

6 (4-ounce) boneless and skinless chicken breast halves

Salt and freshly ground pepper

3 tablespoons oil

2 garlic cloves, minced, plus 1/4 teaspoon oil, or 1 teaspoon prepared minced garlic (see page 17)

1 onion, finely chopped (approximately 1 cup)

1 cup white wine (or 1/2 cup apple jack brandy and 1/2 cup chicken stock)

3 ripe, but firm Bosc pears, peeled, quartered, and sliced

1/2 red bell pepper, thinly sliced

1/2 cup crumbled blue cheese, such as Maytag

3 tablespoons chopped fresh parsley

Salt and freshly ground pepper

SERVES 6

This is a perfect dish to make when you have leftover wild rice. Otherwise, prepare a box of wild rice mix according to the manufacturer's instuctions, omitting the seasoning packet.

✳ Set up three shallow bowls. Place the flour in one, the beaten egg in the second, and the rice mix in the third. Season the chicken with salt and pepper, dredge the chicken in the flour and shake off any excess; then dip the chicken in beaten egg and roll in rice mix to coat evenly.

✳ Preheat the oven to 325° F. In a large sauté pan, cook the chicken in oil over medium-high heat until brown on all sides, approximately 4 to 5 minutes. Transfer the chicken from the pan to a baking sheet and finish cooking in the oven approximately 10 minutes, or until cooked through. Set aside.

✳ Add the garlic to the sauté pan and sauté over low heat for 1 to 2 minutes, or until aromatic. Add the onion and continue sautéing over medium heat until it turns brown, approximately 5 minutes.

✳ Add the wine and deglaze the pan by using a wooden spoon and scraping up the bits that have stuck to the pan. Add the pears and red pepper, bring to a boil. Cover, and cook over medium heat until the liquid is reduced in volume by half and the pears are tender, approximately 5 to 10 minutes. (If the pears are somewhat hard and underripe, add up to another 1/4 cup of wine and cook them for a longer period.)

✳ Remove the pan from the heat, add the blue cheese, and stir until the cheese begins to melt. (You want to have some chunks.) Add 2 tablespoons of parsley, and season with salt and pepper.

✳ To serve, divide the pear mixture evenly and place in the center of each plate. Drizzle some sauce around the pears. Slice each chicken breast on the bias into 3 or 4 medallions and arrange them on top of the pears. Garnish with the remaining parsley.

Dried Apricot, Ham, and Leek-Stuffed Chicken Breasts

SERVES 8

This is a no-fail, sure-fire, prepare-ahead chicken dish from entertaining maven Marlene Sorosky. The chicken breasts are filled with a smoky-fruity stuffing, wrapped in a delicate crust, and topped with an orange-tinged sauce. Reprinted from *Entertaining on the Run* (William Morrow & Co.).

8 (6-ounce) large boneless, skinless chicken breast halves

Marinade

1 1/2 cups orange juice

1 cup chicken stock (homemade or low-sodium canned)

1/2 cup imported dry vermouth or dry white wine

1/4 cup soy sauce

2 tablespoons Dijon mustard

1 tablespoon honey

Stuffing

1/3 cup dried apricots (approximately 10)

2 tablespoons golden raisins

3 medium leeks, cleaned and thickly sliced

4 ounces lean smoked ham or Canadian bacon, cut into 1-inch pieces (approximately 1 cup)

2 tablespoons olive oil

1/3 cup dry bread crumbs, toasted

Crust

3/4 cup chopped shelled pistachios, hazelnuts, or almonds, toasted

1 1/4 cups dry bread crumbs, toasted

Salt and freshly ground pepper

Sauce

1/4 cup heavy cream

4 teaspoons cornstarch

✱ Cut off all fat from chicken. Cut a pocket horizontally into each breast by holding the knife parallel to the counter and cutting back as far as possible without cutting in half. Leave a small edge uncut on 3 sides. Place in a shallow glass casserole or large plastic zipper bag.

✱ Whisk all the marinade ingredients in a medium bowl. Pour 1¼ cups over the chicken, turning to coat all surfaces. Refrigerate for 4 to 12 hours, turning occasionally. Refrigerate the remaining marinade.

✱ To make the stuffing, in a food processor with the metal blade, pulse apricots until coarsely chopped. Add the raisins, leeks, and ham and pulse until diced into ¼-inch pieces. In a large skillet, preferably nonstick, heat the olive oil over moderate heat. Add the apricot mixture and bread crumbs and sauté until leeks are soft and mixture is lightly browned, 5 to 7 minutes. Stir in 2 tablespoons reserved marinade. Cool. (Stuffing may be refrigerated overnight.)

✱ Remove the chicken from the marinade; do not dry. Discard the marinade. Fill each pocket with approximately 2 tablespoons of stuffing. Press the edges to close.

✱ To make the crust, in a pie plate or other shallow dish, stir together the nuts and bread crumbs. Sprinkle the chicken with salt and pepper. Dip both sides into the crumbs, pressing to adhere. Place at least 1 inch apart on a greased or foil-lined and greased baking sheet. Refrigerate until ready to bake. (The chicken may be refrigerated overnight.)

✱ To make the sauce, pour the reserved marinade into a small saucepan. Simmer for 2 to 3 minutes. Remove from the heat. In a small bowl, stir the cream and cornstarch together; then whisk into the sauce. Return the pan to the heat and bring to a boil, whisking constantly. (The sauce may be refrigerated overnight.)

✱ Place the oven rack in the upper third of the oven and preheat to 450° F. Sprinkle the tops of the chicken with the remaining crumbs and spray with no-stick cooking spray. Bake the chicken for 12 to 15 minutes, or until cooked through.

✱ To serve, arrange the chicken breasts on each plate and drizzle with some sauce. Pass the remaining sauce at the table.

Roast Chicken with Mushroom-Pancetta Stuffing

SERVES 6

Rubbing the chicken with lemon prior to cooking makes the skin crisp. The stuffing can be made up to 24 hours ahead. Stuff the bird and put it in the oven 2 hours before meal-time. Reprinted from *Casual Occasions Cookbook* (Weldon Owen).

Stuffing

4 cups cubed day-old bread (approximately 1/2 loaf) or packaged bread cubes

1/2 cup unsalted butter

1/2 pound pancetta, cut into slices 1/4 inch thick and then cut into strips 1/4 inch wide

1 onion, diced (approximately 1 cup)

2 cups sliced fresh mushrooms, wild or cultivated, such as chanterelle or portobello

2 teaspoons chopped fresh thyme

2 teaspoons chopped fresh sage

1/2 to 3/4 cup chicken stock (homemade or low-sodium canned)

Salt and freshly ground pepper

1 large roasting chicken (approximately 6 pounds)

1 lemon, cut in half

Salt and freshly ground pepper

Paprika (optional)

Basting Sauce

1/2 cup olive oil

1/4 cup fresh lemon juice

3 cloves garlic, smashed with the side of a knife

1 tablespoon chopped fresh sage

1 teaspoon chopped fresh thyme

1 teaspoon freshly ground pepper

✳ To make the stuffing, preheat the oven to 300° F. Spread the cubed bread in a large rimmed baking sheet and toast in the oven, stirring from time to time, until dried out, approximately 1 hour.

✳ Meanwhile, in a large sauté pan over medium heat, melt 1/4 cup of the butter. Add the pancetta and sauté until it is nearly crisp, 5 to 8 minutes. Using a slotted spoon, transfer the pancetta to a large bowl and set aside. To the fat remaining in the pan, add the onion and sauté over medium heat until tender and translucent, 8 to 10 minutes. Transfer the onion to the bowl holding the pancetta.

✳ In the same pan, melt the remaining 1/4 cup butter over medium heat. Add the mushrooms and sauté until they give off some liquid, approximately 5 minutes. Stir in the thyme and sage. Transfer the mushrooms and their juices to the bowl holding the pancetta and onion.

✳ Add the bread cubes to the bowl and pour ½ cup of the stock evenly over the top. Toss until all the bread cubes are evenly moistened, adding more stock as needed if the stuffing seems too dry. Season with salt and a generous amount of pepper. Cover and refrigerate for as long as overnight before stuffing the chicken.

✳ Preheat the oven to 375° F. Wipe the bird inside and out with a damp cloth and then with a cut lemon. Rub the cavity lightly with a little salt and pepper. Spoon the stuffing loosely into the body and sew or truss closed. (Place any extra stuffing in a buttered baking dish, cover tightly, and slip it into the oven with the chicken 45 minutes before the chicken is done.) Place the chicken, breast-side down, on a rack in a roasting pan. Sprinkle the flesh with salt, pepper, and a little paprika, if desired.

✳ To make the basting sauce, in a small bowl stir together the olive oil, lemon juice, garlic, sage, thyme, and pepper.

✳ Place the chicken in the oven and roast for 45 minutes, brushing or spooning the basting sauce over the bird every 15 minutes. Turn the chicken, breast-side up, and continue to roast, basting every 15 minutes, until tender and the juices run clear when a thigh is pierced with a skewer, approximately 30 to 45 minutes longer. To test with a roasting thermometer, insert it into the thickest part of the thigh, away from the bone; it should register 180° F.

✳ Remove from the oven, cover loosely with foil, and let rest for approximately 15 minutes. Using a spoon, remove the stuffing from the cavity and place in a serving bowl. Carve the chicken and serve immediately.

Grilled Pepper Steaks
with Cambazola Cheese

3 teaspoons cracked mixed peppercorns

1 tablespoon fresh cilantro, chopped

1 tablespoon molasses

3 tablespoons balsamic vinegar

1 tablespoon prepared minced garlic
   (see page 17)

2 tablespoons roasted garlic oil

1 tablespoon Dijon-style mustard

4 (6-ounce) boneless rib-eye steaks

8 ounces Cambazola cheese, cut into
   8 slices

SERVES 4

This is a decadently delicious dish created by Canadian chef Ted Reader.

✳ In a large shallow bowl, mix together the peppercorns, cilantro, molasses, balsamic vinegar, garlic, oil, and mustard.

✳ Coat the steaks evenly with the spice mixture and let marinate in the bowl for 4 to 6 hours in the refrigerator.

✳ Prepare a grill. Grill the steaks over medium heat for 3 to 4 minutes per side for medium-rare doneness.

✳ Just before the steaks are cooked, top each steak with 2 slices of cheese. Close the barbecue cover and continue to cook for 1 minute, until the cheese starts to melt. Serve immediately.

Meatloaf with Tomato Sauce

SERVES 6

Try serving this
meatloaf with the
Mashed Potatoes with
Escarole, Bacon, and
Roasted Garlic (see
p. 44). You'll need
to roast the garlic
at the same time the
meatloaf is baking.

6-inch-long piece French baguette,
   cut in large 2-inch cubes
1/3 cup half-and-half or low-fat milk
2 cloves garlic, minced, plus 1/4 teaspoon
   oil, or 1 teaspoon prepared minced
   garlic (see page 17)
1 onion, cut into small dice
   (approximately 1 cup)
2 tablespoons chopped fresh parsley
1/2 pound ground beef
1/2 pound ground pork
1/2 pound ground turkey breast

1 egg
1 teaspoon salt
1/2 teaspoon freshly ground pepper
Pinch of nutmeg

Tomato Sauce
1/2 red bell pepper, cut into 1/2-inch dice
1/2 green bell pepper, cut into 1/2-inch dice
1/2 red onion, cut into 1/2-inch dice
1/2 tablespoon olive oil
1 (14-ounce) can chopped tomatoes
1/4 teaspoon freshly ground pepper
1/2 teaspoon dried Italian herb blend

✱ In small bowl, place the bread cubes and the half-and-half or milk, mix well to coat,
and set aside to soak.

✱ In a large sauté pan, heat the garlic over medium heat for 1 to 2 minutes until
golden. Add the onion and continue cooking until translucent, approximately 3 to
5 minutes.

✱ In an electric mixer, place the parsley, ground beef, pork, and turkey, egg, salt,
pepper, nutmeg, and soaked bread and mix until well blended. Add the sautéed garlic
and onion and mix again.

✱ Preheat the oven to 350° F. Lightly grease a 10-inch cake pan with vegetable spray
or oil. Add the meatloaf mixture, cover with plastic wrap, and flatten the meat into
the pan to make a flat, even loaf.

✱ Bake for approximately 35 minutes, or until the top is brown and firm to the touch.
Wait 10 minutes before slicing.

✱ While the meatloaf is baking, make the tomato sauce: In a sauté pan, cook the
peppers and onion in the oil over medium heat for 5 minutes, or until the peppers
begin to soften and the onion becomes translucent. Add the tomatoes, ground pepper,
and herb blend, cover, and simmer for 15 minutes.

✱ To serve, spoon some sauce onto each plate and top with 2 slices of meatloaf. Serve
with a scoop of mashed potatoes and escarole, if desired.

Beer and Lamb Stew with Potatoes and Onion Gravy

1 1/2 pounds lamb stew meat (such as shoulder), cut into large chunks

Salt and freshly ground pepper

1 tablespoon oil

1 1/2 pounds (approximately 5 medium) onions, thinly sliced

4 cloves garlic, minced, plus 1/2 teaspoon oil, or 2 teaspoons prepared minced garlic (see page 17)

1 (12-ounce) bottle dark beer, such as Samuel Adams Double Bock, or your favorite American microbrew

1/3 cup dark molasses or dark Karo syrup

2 bay leaves

2 large sprigs fresh thyme or 1 teaspoon dried thyme

1 sprig of fresh rosemary or 1 teaspoon dried rosemary

1 1/2 pounds (approximately 10 medium) red potatoes, cut into 1 1/2-inch dice

1 teaspoon salt

1/4 cup chopped fresh parsley, for garnish (optional)

SERVES 6

You can also prepare this dish using beef instead of lamb.

✳ Cut the lamb into 2-inch chunks and dry with paper towels. Season on all sides with salt and pepper.

✳ Place a large, nonstick, ovenproof roasting pan over medium high until very hot. Add the lamb chunks and sear, turning to brown all over. Remove from pan.

✳ Preheat the oven to 325° F. Add the oil, onion, and garlic to the pan and sauté over low heat until brown and caramelized, approximately 10 minutes. Increase the heat to medium, add the beer, and stir to scrape up any brown bits from the bottom of the pan. Cook for 2 to 3 minutes until the liquid is slightly reduced.

✳ Add the molasses, bay leaves, thyme, and rosemary to the pan, place the lamb on top of mixture and add the potatoes. Cover and bake in the oven for 30 to 40 minutes, or until the lamb is tender when pierced with a fork.

✳ Remove the lamb and the potatoes from the pan and set aside on a rimmed plate. Bring the braising liquid to a boil and cook over medium-high heat for approximately 10 minutes, or until the sauce has thickened.

✳ To serve, place the potatoes on bottom of an attractive serving dish, top with lamb chunks, and pour the onion gravy on top, partially covering the meat.

Pork Loin Roast in a Port Wine Sauce with Roasted Potato Wedges and Sautéed Spinach

1 tablespoon oil, preferably canola
1 1/2 pounds boneless pork loin

Roasted Potato Wedges

1 1/2 pounds Red Bliss or Russet
   potatoes, cut in 3/4-inch wedges
Salt and freshly ground pepper
1 tablespoon chopped fresh thyme, or
   1 teaspoon dried thyme

Port Wine Sauce

1 large onion, thinly sliced
1 tablespoon brown sugar
1/4 cup currant jelly or red plum jelly
1 1/2 cups port wine
1/2 cup heavy cream

1 tablespoon vinegar, preferably cider
Salt and freshly ground pepper

Sautéed Spinach

1 tablespoon olive oil
4 cloves garlic, minced, plus 1/2 teaspoon
   oil, or 2 teaspoons prepared minced
   garlic (see page 17)
3 pounds fresh spinach, stems removed,
   washed, and drained (or 1 1/2 pounds
   frozen)
1/4 teaspoon nutmeg
1/2 teaspoon salt
1/4 teaspoon freshly ground pepper
1 tablespoon balsamic vinegar

SERVES 6

This is a complete meal that comes together in no time. The potatoes are cooked alongside the pork loin and the spinach can be prepared while the roast is resting.

✱ Preheat the oven to 350° F. In a large sauté pan, heat the oil, then add the pork and brown on all sides, approximately 10 to 15 minutes.

✱ Transfer the pork to a rack placed in a roasting pan and cook in the oven for 20 minutes. Add the potatoes to the roasting pan and continue roasting for another 30 to 40 minutes, or until the potatoes are golden brown on both sides and the internal temperature of the roast reaches 150 to 165° F. Remove from the oven and let the roast rest.

✱ To make the port wine sauce, add the onion and brown sugar to the original sauté pan and cook over medium-low heat until they caramelize, approximately 10 minutes. Add the jelly and the port to the pan and simmer until the liquid reduces in volume by one half, approximately 10 to 12 minutes. Add the heavy cream and continue cooking over low heat until the sauce reduces by one third, and coats the back of a spoon. Stir in the vinegar and season with salt and pepper.

✱ In a large deep pot with a tight fitting lid, sauté the garlic in the oil over low heat until aromatic, approximately 1 to 2 minutes. Add the spinach, cover, and cook for approximately 2 minutes, or until wilted and turned bright green. Remove the pan from the heat, uncover, and stir in the nutmeg, salt, pepper, and vinegar.

✱ To serve, divide the spinach evenly and place to one side of each plate. Slice the pork on the bias into 1/4-inch-thick slices and fan 2 to 3 slices next to the spinach. Arrange the potatoes next to the pork and drizzle the sauce all over.

Pork Loin in a Mustard Sauce with Mixed Vegetables

SERVES 6

This sauce gets its rich flavor from the combination of mustards. However, in a pinch, you can use 4 tablespoons of Dijon-style mustard.

1 1/2 pounds boneless pork loin
1 tablespoon freshly cracked black pepper
1 tablespoon vegetable oil

Mustard Sauce
2 cloves garlic, minced, plus 1/4 teaspoon
   oil, or 1 teaspoon prepared minced
   garlic (see page 17)
1 tablespoon chili powder
1 cup chicken stock (homemade or
   low-sodium canned)
2 tablespoons brown mustard
2 tablespoons coarse-grain mustard
1/2 cup dark Karo syrup

1/2 teaspoon salt
1 1/2 cups (approximately 2 small) onions,
   cut into large dice

Mixed Vegetables
1 pound yellow squash, cut in half
   lengthwise, then sliced into 1/4-inch
   half moons
1 tablespoon olive oil
8 ounces sugar snap peas
1 (15-ounce) can red kidney beans,
   rinsed and drained
2 tablespoons chopped fresh parsley
Salt and freshly ground pepper

✱ Roll the pork loin in the cracked pepper. In a large, ovenproof sauté pan, heat the oil, add the loin, and brown on all sides, approximately 10 minutes. Remove the loin from the pan and set aside.

✱ Preheat the oven to 350° F. Add the garlic and chili powder to the pan and sauté over medium-low heat until golden, approximately 2 minutes. Add the chicken stock, mustards, Karo syrup, salt, and onions and simmer for 2 minutes.

✱ Return the roast to the sauté pan, cover, and finish cooking in the oven for 45 minutes, or until the internal temperature of the loin reaches 150 to 165° F. Remove from the oven and let the roast rest for 10 minutes before slicing.

✱ While the roast is resting, prepare the vegetables. In a large sauté pan, sauté the squash in the oil over high heat for 1 minute, then add the peas and cook for another 2 minutes, or until the peas are slightly cooked but still firm to the bite. Add the beans and cook for 1 minute or until warmed through. Stir in the parsley and season with salt and pepper to taste.

✱ To serve, slice the pork on the bias into 1/4-inch-thick slices and fan 3 slices across each plate. Arrange the vegetables around the pork and drizzle the sauce all over.

Pork Tenderloin with Molasses, Bacon, and Porcini Vinaigrette

Porcini Oil

1 ounce dried porcini mushrooms

1 cup olive oil

6 tablespoons porcini oil (from above) or good quality olive oil

2 pounds pork tenderloin

Salt and freshly ground pepper

½ pound bacon, cut into ¼-inch dice

1 tablespoon finely chopped garlic

1 teaspoon finely chopped rosemary or ½ teaspoon dried rosemary

⅓ cup balsamic vinegar

2 tablespoons dark molasses

1 tablespoon finely chopped fresh flat-leaf parsley

SERVES 4

This *agro dolci* (sweet and sour) pork dish was created by Michael Chiarello. You can find porcini-flavored olive oil in specialty gourmet stores or make your own, following the recipe included here. Reprinted from *Flavored Oils* (Chronicle Books).

✳ To make your own porcini oil, place the mushrooms in a food processor fitted with a metal blade and chop until fine. Place in a pot with the oil and heat until the mixture begins to bubble. Let cook 10 to 15 seconds and remove from heat. Swirl until just warm. Strain into a bowl through 4 layers of cheesecloth. Squeeze well to extract as much oil as possible. Pour into a sterilized jar or bottle, seal tightly, refrigerate, and use within 1 week. Makes approximately ¾ cup porcini oil.

✳ Preheat the oven to 400° F. Heat 3 tablespoons of the porcini oil in a heavy, oven-proof pan over medium-high heat until hot. Season the pork with salt and pepper and then add to the pan and brown on all sides, approximately 3 to 5 minutes. Transfer the pan to the oven and roast until the internal temperature reaches 165° F, approximately 15 minutes.

✳ When the pork has cooked, transfer it to a rimmed platter and cover to keep warm. Pour the cooking juices from the pan over the meat. Return the pan to medium heat, add the bacon, and cook until crisp, approximately 8 to 10 minutes. Drain off and discard all but 2 tablespoons of fat from the pan. Add the garlic and sauté over medium-high heat until light brown. Add the rosemary, remove from the heat, add the vinegar, and stir up all the brown bits that have stuck to the bottom of the pan. Add the molasses and stir well.

✳ To finish the sauce, return the pan to the heat and stir in the meat juices that have accumulated around the meat. Add the parsley and remaining 3 tablespoons porcini oil. Cover to keep warm.

✳ To serve, slice the pork on the bias into ¼-inch-thick slices and fan 3 slices across each plate. Spoon the sauce over the meat.

Marinated Shrimp with Soft Polenta and Asparagus

Marinade

¹/₂ serrano chili, seeded

2 cloves garlic, minced, plus ¹/₄ teaspoon oil, or 1 teaspoon prepared minced garlic (see page 17)

¹/₂ cup dry sherry or dry white wine

¹/₄ cup olive oil

¹/₄ cup cider vinegar or rice vinegar

¹/₄ cup chopped onion

1 teaspoon chili powder

¹/₂ teaspoon salt

2 large tomatoes, peeled, seeded, and cut into 1-inch wedges

1 ¹/₂ pounds (30 to 40 medium) shrimp, peeled and deveined if necessary

Polenta

7 cups water

1 ¹/₂ teaspoons salt

4 cloves garlic, minced, plus ¹/₂ teaspoon oil, or 2 teaspoons prepared minced garlic (see page 17)

2 cup yellow or white coarse cornmeal

1 tablespoon unsalted butter

¹/₂ cup grated Parmesan cheese

2 tablespoons chopped fresh cilantro

18 ounces asparagus tips, cut on the bias into 3-inch-long pieces

SERVES 6

Don't be fooled by the number of ingredients, this dish is actually quite easy and the results are well worth it. You may also serve the polenta hard and cut into traingles (see photograph).

✳ Place all the marinade ingredients except the tomatoes in a food processor fitted with the metal blade and process until smooth.

✳ Place the shrimp in a large bowl and pour the marinade over them, tossing to coat well. Place the shrimp in the refrigerator to marinate for 20 minutes.

✳ While the shrimp are marinating, make the polenta: Preheat the oven to 325° F. Bring the water, salt, and garlic to a boil in an ovenproof sauce pot. Slowly whisk in the cornmeal in a slow, steady stream. Bring to boil, cover with a tight-fitting lid, and then place the pot in the oven to finish cooking for 20 minutes, or until the polenta is thick and creamy. Remove from the oven and keep warm.

✳ Preheat the oven to 325° F. With a slotted spoon, remove the shrimp from the marinade, shaking off any excess, and place on baking sheet. Bake for approximately 6 to 8 minutes, or until the shrimp turn pink and are firm to the touch but not tough.

✳ Pour the reserved marinade into a saucepan, add the tomato wedges, and simmer over low heat for 5 minutes. Set aside.

✳ Just before serving, steam the asparagus until al dente, approximately 3 to 5 minutes. Stir the butter, cheese, and cilantro into the polenta.

✳ To serve, place approximately 1 cup polenta in the center of each plate. Arrange the asparagus, shrimp, and tomato around the polenta and pour the sauce around the edges.

Cedar-Planked Salmon

SERVES 4

Leading Vancouver chef, Margaret Chisholm, brought us this recipe, which uses an old Native American technique of cooking fish on a cedar plank that infuses it with wonderful flavor. For convenience, ask your fishmonger to remove the skin and bones for you.

1 plank of cedar (see note), approximately 18 inches long x 8 inches wide

3 tablespoons olive oil

1 (2-pound) side of salmon

Coarse sea salt

Freshly ground pepper

✻ Preheat the oven to 350° F. Very lightly brush the plank with a bit of the oil. Place the plank in the oven until it begins to brown slightly and becomes warm, approximately 10 to 15 minutes.

✻ Meanwhile, remove the skin from the salmon and, using tweezers, pluck out the small pin bones. Brush the salmon with the remaining oil. Season both sides with salt and pepper.

✻ Remove the heated plank from the oven. Place the salmon on the plank, place the plank back into the oven, and roast the fish for 15 to 20 minutes, or until barely done in the thickest part. Serve immediately.

Note: Cedar plank is available at the lumber yard or through mail order—check the listing in the back of cooking magazines for a supplier. Just be sure the wood has not been chemically treated.

New England-Style Pot-au-Feu

3 cloves garlic, cut into slivers

2 tablespoons olive oil

1 onion, thinly sliced

1 cup thinly sliced celery

1 cup thinly sliced fennel

1 cup thinly sliced carrots

1 cup thinly sliced leeks (white parts only)

1/2 cup green peas

3 cups chicken stock (homemade or
   low-sodium canned), or clam juice

10 ounces (6 small) Yukon Gold potatoes,
   quartered

1 cup white wine

1 tablespoon fresh thyme leaves,
   stems removed, plus 6 additional
   thyme sprigs for garnish

2 large tomatoes, peeled, seeded, and
   juice removed (flesh only)

8 ounces quality crab meat such as
   snow crab, king crab, or stone crab

SERVES 6

An updated, seafood
version of the tradi-
tional family-style
boiled dinner, this is
one-pot cooking at
its best.

✱ In a large stock pot or Dutch oven, sauté the garlic in oil over low heat until aromatic, approximately 1 to 2 minutes. Add the onion, celery, fennel, carrots, leeks,
peas, chicken stock, potatoes, wine, and thyme and simmer until the vegetables are
tender, but not mushy, approximately 20 minutes.

✱ Place the tomatoes and the crab lumps on top of the vegetables and simmer for
another 2 minutes to warm the crab. (Do not overcook the crab.)

✱ To serve, spoon the stew into large bowls and garnish with fresh thyme sprigs.

Eggplant, Two-Tomato, and Pesto Torte

SERVES 10

The cookbook author and entertaining expert, Marlene Sorosky, says the only way to enjoy your own dinner parties is to do-ahead, make-ahead, be-ahead. This torte may be kept covered in the refrigerator up to 2 days or frozen up to 1 month. The torte is best baked 1 day before serving and reheated, uncovered, at 400° F for 15 to 20 minutes. Reprinted from *Entertaining on the Run* (William Morrow & Co.).

3 medium eggplants (3 to 3 1/2 pounds total)
1/4 cup olive oil, or more

Tomato Sauce

1 tablespoon olive oil
1 large onion, chopped
1/3 cup sun-dried tomatoes, cut with scissors into small pieces
1 (28-ounce) can Italian-style plum tomatoes, drained
2 small zucchini, sliced very thinly (approximately 1/2 pound)

1 teaspoon dried oregano or 1 tablespoon chopped fresh oregano leaves
1 tablespoon raspberry vinegar
Salt and freshly ground pepper

Pesto Sauce

2 large garlic cloves, peeled
2 cups (lightly packed) fresh basil leaves
1/4 cup shredded Parmesan cheese

1 cup dry bread crumbs
6 ounces sliced Monterey Jack or mozzarella cheese
3 tablespoons shredded Parmesan cheese
Fresh basil leaves, for garnish (optional)

✷ Preheat the oven to 400° F.

✷ Cut the ends off the eggplant, peel, and slice crosswise into 1/4- to 1/3-inch thick slices. Cover 2 baking sheets with heavy foil and generously brush with olive oil. Arrange the eggplant slices close together in one layer on the sheets and brush the tops with olive oil. Bake the eggplant for 12 minutes. Rotate the baking sheets and bake 12 to 15 minutes longer, or until the eggplant is very soft and the bottoms are lightly browned. Remove from the oven and loosen from baking sheet with a spatula; leave on the baking sheets until cool enough to handle.

✷ While the eggplant is baking, make the tomato sauce: In a large skillet over medium-high heat, heat the olive oil. Add the onion and sauté, stirring, for 2 minutes. Cover the pan with a sheet of wax paper and a lid and cook over low heat, stirring occasionally, until the onion is soft but not brown, approximately 10 minutes.

✷ Meanwhile, place the sun-dried tomatoes in a 2-cup microwave measure with 1 cup water. Cover with plastic wrap and microwave on High for 3 to 4 minutes, or until very soft. Alternatively, bring a small pot of water to a boil and add the dry tomatoes. Simmer gently for 1 minute, then remove from the heat and set aside for 5 minutes, or until soft. Transfer the tomatoes to a food processor fitted with the metal blade, add ¼ cup of the liquid, and process until puréed. Cut the canned tomatoes in half, squeeze out the seeds, and remove any hard stems. Add to the food processor and pulse until chunky. Transfer the tomato purée back to the skillet with the onions. Add the zucchini, oregano, vinegar, and salt and pepper to taste. Cook, uncovered, over medium heat, stirring occasionally, until zucchini is soft, approximately 5 to 7 minutes.

✳ To make the pesto sauce, place the garlic in a food processor fitted with the metal blade and mince. Add the basil and Parmesan and purée. Add 3 tablespoons of water and pulse to incorporate. Set aside.

✳ To assemble the torte, grease or spray a 9-inch springform pan. Sprinkle the bread crumbs over the bottom. Spoon 1 cup of tomato sauce over the crumbs; it will not cover them. Arrange one-third of the eggplant over the sauce. Spread with 1 cup tomato sauce, then layer with half the sliced cheese, half the pesto, and another third of the eggplant. Continue layering in the same order: 1 cup of tomato sauce, the remaining cheese, pesto, eggplant, and tomato sauce.

✳ Preheat the oven to 400° F. Wrap the bottom of the springform pan in heavy foil and place on a baking sheet. Bake, covered with foil, in the center of the oven until heated through, 40 minutes if the torte is at room temperature, 50 to 60 minutes if cold.

✳ Sprinkle with Parmesan cheese and bake, uncovered, for 10 minutes. Let stand 15 minutes before serving.

✳ To serve, remove the sides of the springform and place the torte on a serving platter. Garnish with fresh basil leaves, if desired.

Eggplant Casserole

Filling

3 cups chicken stock (homemade or
    low-sodium canned)

1 cup (7 ounces) dry barley

8 ounces part-skim mozzarella cheese, cut
    into small dice (approximately 2 cups)

4 ounces Parmesan cheese, grated
    (approximately 1 cup)

Eggplant

2 pounds (approximately 1 medium)
    eggplant, unpeeled, cut into $1/4$-inch-
    thick slices

2 tablespoons olive oil

Tomato Sauce

4 cloves garlic, minced, plus $1/2$ teaspoon
    oil, or 2 teaspoons prepared minced
    garlic (see page 17)

1 tablespoon olive oil

1 medium onion, thinly sliced
    (approximately 1 cup)

1 (16-ounce) can diced or crushed tomatoes

1 tablespoon tomato paste

1 bay leaf

1 teaspoon fresh rosemary, minced, or
    $1/4$ teaspoon dried rosemary

Pinch of sugar

Pinch of cayenne pepper

SERVES 6

This meatless
casserole can be
prepared several
hours ahead or the
day before, and then
baked off when you
are ready to serve
it. If you're pressed
for time, you can
use a storebought
tomato sauce.

✶ To make the filling, in a medium pot bring the chicken stock to boil. Add the barley, cover, bring to boil again, then reduce the heat to low and simmer for 35 to 40 minutes. When the barley is done, fold in the cheeses and mix well.

✶ Meanwhile, prepare the eggplant. Prepare a grill or preheat the broiler. Brush the eggplant slices with the oil and grill or broil until golden on both sides, approximately 3 to 5 minutes on each side, or until the eggplant begins to soften and is slightly browned. Transfer to a plate and set aside.

✶ To make the tomato sauce, lightly sauté the garlic in oil in a sauté pan over low heat for 1 to 2 minutes, or until aromatic. Add the onion and cook until translucent, approximately 3 to 5 minutes. Add the tomatoes, tomato paste, bay leaf, rosemary, sugar, and cayenne and continue to cook for 10 minutes. Remove the bay leaf and set the sauce aside.

✶ Preheat the oven to 350° F. Lightly grease a 9- x 12-inch casserole dish with vegetable oil.

✶ To assemble the casserole, arrange half of the eggplant slices evenly on the bottom of the dish. Spread half the filling over the eggplant, and cover with half the tomato sauce. Top with another layer of eggplant, spread the remaining filling on top, and cover with a final layer of tomato sauce.

✶ Place the casserole dish on a baking sheet and bake for 35 minutes, or until bubbly. Remove from the oven and allow to cool for 10 to 15 minutes before slicing.

Four-Bean Meatless Chili

1 cup partially cooked dry bulgur

3 cups boiling water

Chili

2 tablespoons olive oil

4 garlic cloves, minced, plus 1/2 teaspoon oil, or 2 teaspoons prepared minced garlic (see page 17)

3 onions, cut into 1/2-inch dice

10 ounces (3 cups) mushrooms of your choice, cut into 1/2-inch dice

2 teaspoons chili powder

1 teaspoon ground ancho chili or chopped jalapeño

1 teaspoon ground cumin

1/2 teaspoon red pepper flakes

1 teaspoon paprika

2 (16-ounce) cans chopped tomatoes

4 (15-ounce) cans of different beans (such as white and red kidney, pinto, and black), rinsed and drained

1 3/4 cups chicken stock (homemade or low-sodium canned)

1 tablespoon cider or red wine vinegar

1 teaspoon salt

1/4 cup fresh cilantro leaves, for garnish (optional)

SERVES 6

With the versatile taste that comes from using four different kinds of beans you won't miss the meat in this chili. If you haven't experimented with bulgur, you'll find it an incredibly easy-to-make grain that goes wonderfully well with chili.

✳ Rinse the bulgur under cold running water to remove any dust. Drain, then put the bulgur in a bowl, add the boiling water, and let soak for 30 minutes. If neccessary, drain the bulgur and squeeze to remove excess moisture. Fluff the grains with a fork. Set aside.

✳ While the bulgur is soaking, make the chili: In a Dutch oven, heat the oil and sauté the garlic and onions together over medium heat until translucent, approximately 3 to 5 minutes. Add the mushrooms and spices and cook for 5 minutes, or until browned. Add the tomatoes, beans, and stock, cover, and simmer for 15 minutes to warm all the ingredients through. Do not excessively stir the mixture or you will mash the beans. Stir in the vinegar and salt.

✳ To serve, spoon the chili into large soup plates. Mound 1/2 cup of cooked bulgur in the center of each and garnish with whole cilantro leaves, if desired.

Basic Cheese Quesadillas Several Ways

SERVES 4

These quesadillas are low in fat, quick to prepare, and can be enhanced by any number of additional fillings. Here, Martha Rose Schulman provides a basic recipe and a gourmet variation. Both versions can be assembled, covered with plastic wrap, and refrigerated for several hours ahead of time. The quesadillas can be cooked on the stove top or in the oven. Reprinted from *Mexican Light* (Bantam Books).

1 cup nonfat cottage cheese
1 ¹/₂ ounces Monterey Jack, mild or sharp white Cheddar, or Parmesan cheese, or a combination, grated (approximately ¹/₃ cup)

8 corn tortillas
Green or red salsa, for serving

✳ In a food processor fitted with the metal blade, blend together the cottage cheese and grated cheese until completely smooth.

✳ **To prepare the quesadillas using the oven,** preheat the oven to 400° F. Heat the tortillas one at a time, turning in a dry skillet over medium-high heat until flexible. Spread 2 tablespoons of the cheese mixture over each tortilla, leaving a ¹/₂-inch border around the edge, and fold the tortilla over. Place on an unoiled baking sheet. Heat, fill, and fold all the tortillas in this way. Heat through in the hot oven for 10 minutes, until the cheese melts and the tortillas just begin to crisp and curl up slightly on top. Transfer to plates and serve hot, passing salsa to spoon over the top.

✳ **To prepare the quesadillas using the stove top,** heat the tortillas, 2 or 3 at a time, in a dry skillet over medium-high heat until flexible. Spread 2 tablespoons of the cheese mixture over each tortilla, leaving a ¹/₂-inch border around the edge, and fold the tortilla over. Heat through, turning the folded tortilla over from time to time, until the cheese melts, approximately 5 to 8 minutes. Don't worry if some of the cheese runs out onto the pan (it probably will). Transfer to plates and serve hot, passing salsa to spoon over the top.

✳ **To prepare the quesadillas using the microwave,** wrap 4 tortillas in microwave-safe plastic wrap, a dampened towel, or wax paper and heat for 30 seconds to 1 minute in the microwave, until flexible. Spread 2 tablespoons of the cheese mixture over each tortilla, leaving a ¹/₂-inch border around the edge, and fold the tortilla over. Place on a plate or plates and cover with plastic, paper towel, or wax paper. Repeat with the next 4 tortillas. Heat all the quesadillas through in the microwave for 2 minutes, uncover, and serve hot, passing salsa to spoon over the top.

Quesadillas with Goat Cheese, Roasted Peppers, and Black Beans

2 medium red bell peppers or pimentos

2 large garlic cloves, minced or pressed

2 ounces goat cheese, crumbled
 (approximately $1/2$ cup)

$3/4$ cup nonfat cottage cheese

Salt and freshly ground pepper

2 cups cooked black beans in their
 cooking liquid, or 2 (15-ounce) cans
 black beans

8 corn tortillas

1 cup tomato salsa (homemade or
 prepared)

✳ To roast peppers, prepare a grill or preheat the broiler. Roast the peppers either directly over a gas flame or under a broiler, turning often until uniformly charred. When the peppers are blackened on all sides, transfer to a plastic bag, seal, and cool. Remove the charred skin, rinse, and pat dry. Remove the seeds and veins.

✳ In a food processor fitted with the metal blade, chop the garlic cloves. Add the roasted peppers (or pimentos) and process to a coarse purée. Add the goat cheese and cottage cheese and blend until smooth. Season with salt and pepper.

✳ Heat the beans in a saucepan over medium heat until simmering.

✳ Heat the tortillas, 1 or 2 at a time, in a dry skillet, following the instructions for the basic quesadillas. Transfer to plates and serve hot, passing salsa to spoon over the top.

SERVES 4

Three distinct savory flavors merge here into a luscious, filling quesadilla. These taste so rich that you won't believe they're low in fat. Reprinted from *Mexican Light* (Bantam Books).

Polenta Casserole with Mushroom Sauce

SERVES 6

The method of making polenta revealed in this recipe eliminates the need to stir it constantly. For a fancier presentation, make individual casseroles (see photograph).

Polenta

6 cups water

1 teaspoon salt

2 cloves garlic, minced, plus ¹/₄ teaspoon oil, or 1 teaspoon prepared minced garlic (see page 17)

2 cups coarse yellow cornmeal

Mushroom Sauce

1 ounce assorted dried mushrooms (such as porcini, chanterelles, or cèpes)

1 cup boiling water

2 cloves garlic, minced, plus ¹/₄ teaspoon oil, or 1 teaspoon prepared minced garlic (see page 17)

2 tablespoons olive oil

1 onion, cut into small dice

1 pound white mushrooms, cut into ¹/₃-inch slices

¹/₂ cup half-and-half

¹/₄ teaspoon freshly ground pepper

3 tablespoons chopped fresh parsley

1 cup grated pecorino cheese

1 cup grated mozzarella cheese

✳ To make the polenta, preheat the oven to 325° F. Bring the water, salt, and garlic to a boil in an ovenproof pot. Slowly whisk in the cornmeal in a steady stream. Bring to boil, cover with a tight-fitting lid, and then place the pot in the oven for 20 minutes to finish cooking or until thick and creamy.

✳ Pour the polenta onto a 12- x 18-inch lightly greased or nonstick baking sheet and spread evenly. Cover with plastic wrap and refrigerate for 40 minutes, or until cold.

✳ While the polenta is cooling, make mushroom sauce: In small bowl, soak the dried mushrooms in boiling water until soft, approximately 30 minutes. When soft, strain and reserve the soaking liquid.

✳ In large sauté pan, sauté the garlic in oil over medium-low heat until golden, approximately 1 to 2 minutes. Add the onion and continue sautéing until brown, approximately 5 minutes. Add the dried and fresh mushrooms and sauté for an additional 5 minutes. Add the half-and-half, pepper, and reserved mushroom water and cook over medium heat until the sauce is thickened and coats the back of a spoon. Remove from the heat and stir in the parsley.

✳ Preheat the oven to 375° F. To layer the casserole, cut the cooled polenta in half, widthwise. Lightly grease a 9- x 12-inch casserole dish. Line the bottom of the casserole dish with one of the polenta halves. Spread half of the mushroom sauce across the polenta. Mix together the cheeses and evenly distribute half on top. Place the second half of the polenta on top. Spoon the remaining mushroom sauce down the center of the polenta and sprinkle the entire casserole with the remaining cheese.

✳ Bake for 20 minutes, or until bubbly. Let cool for 15 minutes before serving.

DESSERTS

Caramel-Nut Popcorn

3 quarts freshly popped corn
   (approximately 1/2 cup unpopped)

1 cup unsalted roasted cashews

1 cup salted roasted macadamia nuts

1 cup whole almonds or pecan halves

1 cup firmly packed dark brown sugar

1/2 cup light corn syrup

1/2 cup unsalted butter

1 tablespoon finely grated orange zest

1/2 teaspoon salt

1 teaspoon vanilla extract

1/2 teaspoon baking soda

✳ Preheat the oven to 250° F. Butter a large roasting pan. Combine the popped corn and nuts in the prepared pan, mixing well. Place in the oven while preparing the glaze.

✳ In a large heavy saucepan over medium heat, combine the brown sugar, corn syrup, butter, orange zest, and salt. Bring to a boil, stirring constantly until the sugar dissolves. Boil for 4 minutes without stirring. Remove from the heat and mix in the vanilla and baking soda. Gradually pour the glaze over the popped corn mixture, stirring to coat well.

✳ Bake until dry, stirring occasionally, approximately 1 hour. Remove from the oven. Using a metal spatula, free the popcorn from the bottom of the pan. Let cool completely in the pan.

✳ Break into clumps. Store in an airtight container at room temperature for up to 1 week.

**MAKES
APPROXIMATELY
4 QUARTS**

This snack, created by Kristine Kidd, is likely the most luxurious popcorn you could ever want. You can substitute for these nuts any of your favorite nuts. Reprinted from *Gifts from the Kitchen: Williams-Sonoma Kitchen Library* (Time Life).

Chocolate Chip Biscotti

MAKES APPROXIMATELY 3 DOZEN COOKIES

In these biscotti the nutty flavors of chocolate, rolled oats, and almonds are combined. For a variation, omit the chocolate chips and add ¼ cup of cocoa powder and 6 ounces of chocolate-covered raisins.

1/4 cup vegetable oil
1 1/2 cups tightly packed brown sugar
2 eggs
1 teaspoon instant coffee diluted in
    1/4 cup hot water
1 teaspoon vanilla extract
2 1/2 cups all-purpose flour

1 cup old-fashioned rolled oats,
    finely ground in food processor or
    coffee grinder
1 1/2 teaspoons baking powder
1/2 teaspoon salt
1/2 cup blanched slivered almonds, toasted
3/4 cup chocolate chips

✳ Preheat the oven to 375° F. Lightly grease a nonstick baking sheet.

✳ In a bowl, using an electric mixer, blend the oil, brown sugar, eggs, coffee, and vanilla extract together.

✳ In a separate bowl, mix together the flour, ground oats, baking powder, and salt. Add the flour mixture to the wet mixture, mixing until smooth. Using a wooden spoon, fold in the nuts and chocolate chips.

✳ Lightly flour your hands, divide the dough into 2 equal parts and shape each part into 2 logs, approximately 2 inches in diameter. Place the logs on the baking sheet, spacing them well apart, and bake in the oven for 25 minutes, or until firm to the touch. Let cool for 10 minutes. Leave the oven set at 350° F.

✳ Using a spatula, carefully transfer the logs to a work surface. Using a serrated knife, cut on the diagonal into slices ½ inch thick. Return the slices cut-side down to the baking sheet. Bake until brown, approximately 20 minutes, or until the biscotti are dry and crisp.

✳ Transfer the cookies to wire racks to cool. Store in an airtight container at room temperature for up to 2 weeks.

Cranberry-Almond Biscotti

1 cup dried cranberries

2 eggs

3/4 cup sugar, plus extra for topping

1/2 cup vegetable oil

2 tablespoons finely grated orange zest

1 teaspoon ground cinnamon

1 1/4 teaspoons baking powder

1 teaspoon pure vanilla extract

1/2 teaspoon almond extract

1/4 teaspoon salt

2 cups all-purpose flour, or as needed

1 cup slivered blanched almonds

✳ Preheat the oven to 350° F. Place the cranberries in a bowl with hot water to cover and let stand for 10 minutes. Drain and set aside.

✳ In a large bowl, combine the eggs, 3/4 cup sugar, the oil, orange zest, cinnamon, baking powder, vanilla and almond extracts, and salt. Whisk to blend. Add the flour, almonds, and cranberries and stir until a dough forms. Turn out onto a heavily floured surface and knead until smooth, adding more flour if the dough is too sticky to work, approximately 20 turns. Divide the dough in half.

✳ Continuing to work on the floured surface, form each half into a log 2 inches in diameter. Carefully transfer the logs to an ungreased baking sheet, spacing them well apart. Sprinkle the tops with sugar.

✳ Bake until golden brown and firm to the touch, approximately 30 minutes. Let cool for 10 minutes. Leave the oven set at 350° F.

✳ Using a spatula, carefully transfer the logs to a work surface. Using a serrated knife, cut on the diagonal into slices 1/2 inch thick. Return the slices cut-side down to the baking sheet. Bake until brown, approximately 20 minutes, or until the biscotti are dry and crisp.

✳ Transfer the cookies to wire racks to cool. Store in an airtight container at room temperature for up to 2 weeks.

MAKES APPROXIMATELY 3 DOZEN COOKIES

Kristine Kidd provides this variation of the classic biscotti for the holidays. They look great when presented in a glass jar, or in a twist-tie-sealed bag tucked inside a pretty gift bag. Reprinted from *Cookies and Biscotti: Williams-Sonoma Kitchen Library* (Time Life).

Vanilla and Walnut Shortbread Hearts

MAKES APPROXIMATELY 20 COOKIES

Bon Appetit editor, Kristine Kidd, believes this is the best shortbread she's ever tried. These festive cookies look pretty whether left plain, sprinkled with colored crystals, or decorated with confectioners' sugar icing. Reprinted from *Cookies and Biscotti: Williams-Sonoma Kitchen Library* (Time Life).

1 cup all-purpose flour
2 1/2 tablespoons cornstarch
1/8 teaspoon salt
1/3 cup granulated sugar

1/2 cup unsalted butter, at room temperature
1 teaspoon pure vanilla extract
1/2 cup walnuts, finely chopped

✻ Preheat the oven to 350° F.

✻ In a small bowl, sift together the flour, cornstarch, and salt; set aside.

✻ In a large bowl, combine the sugar, butter, and vanilla. Using an electric mixer set on High, beat the sugar and butter mixture until light and fluffy. Reduce the speed to Low, add the flour mixture and beat until the mixture begins to gather together into a rough dough. Stir in the walnuts.

✻ Turn out the dough onto a sheet of waxed paper. Gather into a ball, then flatten into a disc. Cover with another sheet of waxed paper. Roll out the dough ¼-inch thick. Remove the top sheet of waxed paper, and using a heart-shaped cookie cutter 3 inches in diameter, cut out cookies. Transfer the cookies to an ungreased baking sheet, spacing them ½ inch apart. Gather up the scraps into a flat disc, reroll the dough, and cut out additional cookies. Transfer to the baking sheet.

✻ Bake until the cookies are firm to the touch and just beginning to color, approximately 20 minutes. Transfer the cookies to wire racks to cool. Store in an airtight container at room temperature for up to 2 weeks.

Chocolate-Chipped Vanilla Scones

1 3/4 cups all-purpose flour

1/3 cup confectioners' sugar

2 teaspoons baking powder

1/2 teaspoon salt

1/2 cup cold unsalted butter, cut into
   12 pieces

1/2 cup semisweet chocolate chips

2/3 cup plus 1 teaspoon whipping cream,
   at room temperature

1 tablespoon plus 1/4 teaspoon pure
   vanilla extract

1 teaspoon sugar

❋ Preheat the oven to 400° F. Grease a large baking sheet; set aside.

❋ **To make the dough by hand,** in a large bowl, combine the flour, sugar, baking powder, and salt. Using a pastry cutter or 2 knives, cut the butter into the mixture until it resembles very coarse crumbs. Stir in the chocolate chips. Combine 2/3 cup of the cream and 1 tablespoon vanilla; add to the flour mixture, stirring only until the dry ingredients are moistened.

❋ **To make the dough in a food processor,** place the flour, sugar, baking powder, and salt in the work bowl fitted with the metal blade; process for 15 seconds. Add the butter and chocolate chips; pulse on and off quickly just until the mixture resembles very coarse crumbs. Combine 2/3 cup of the cream and 1 tablespoon vanilla; add to the flour mixture, and pulse on and off only until the dry ingredients are moistened. Do not overprocess.

❋ Turn the dough out onto a generously floured work surface. Gently press the dough together and pat into a circle approximately 3/4-inch thick and 7 1/2 inches in diameter. In a small bowl, combine the remaining 1 teaspoon of cream and 1/4 teaspoon vanilla. Brush the cream mixture over the top of the dough; sprinkle with the sugar.

❋ Using a sharp knife, cut the dough circle into 8 wedges. Place the wedges, 2 inches apart, on the prepared baking sheet. Bake for 15 minutes, or until golden brown.

❋ Transfer the scones to wire racks to cool. Store in an airtight container at room temperature.

MAKES 8 SCONES

Sharon Tyler Herbst, the creator of these scones, reminds us that the most important thing to remember when making quick breads like these is to handle them with care. Overworking the dough will produce a dense, heavy, or tough bread. For the flakiest scones, the butter should be cold and cut into 3/8-inch chunks. Reprinted from *The Food Lover's Guide to Chocolate and Vanilla* (William Morrow & Co.).

Drunken Bananas
with Candied Spiced Almonds

Candied Spiced Almonds

1 tablespoon, plus 1/2 teaspoon
    unsalted butter

2 tablespoons sugar

1/2 cup slivered almonds

1 pinch cayenne pepper

1 pinch ground cinnamon

1 pinch chili powder

1 squirt of lemon juice

Caramel Sauce

1/2 cup maple syrup or brown sugar

1/4 cup dark rum or bourbon

2 tablespoons unsalted butter

Pinch of salt

1/4 cup evaporated skim milk

6 bananas, sliced on a deep bias into
    2-inch chunks

Frozen vanilla yogurt or ice cream,
    for garnish (optional)

SERVES 6

This low-fat dessert has tremendous depth of flavor and texture with its warm, soft bananas, crunchy, sweet nuts, and the cool frozen yogurt. Be extremely careful when working with the caramel sauce, which should never come in contact with your skin. Also be sure to remove the pan from the heat before lighting the bourbon.

✱ To make the candied spiced almonds, place 1 tablespoon of the butter and the sugar in a small sauce pot and cook over low heat, stirring constantly, until melted and golden brown.

✱ In a small bowl, toss the almonds with the cayenne, cinnamon, and chili powder. Add the spiced nuts to the melted sugar and cook over low heat, stirring constantly, until the nuts are golden brown, approximately 5 to 7 minutes. Remove from the heat, and stir in the remaining 1/2 teaspoon butter and lemon juice. Transfer the candied nuts to a plate and let cool.

✱ To make the caramel sauce, in large skillet cook the maple syrup over medium heat until it has reduced in volume by half. (If using brown sugar, just heat it through before adding the rum or bourbon.) Pour in the bourbon, remove from the heat, and then ignite the sauce with a lighted match. (The flame should burn out after a few seconds.) Return the pan to the heat and continue to cook over medium heat until the sauce is reduced to light caramel consistency.

✱ Remove the pan from the heat. Add the butter, salt, and milk and stir until fully incorporated and smooth. Set aside.

✱ Lightly grease the bananas with vegetable spray or melted butter. Place a sauté pan over high heat until it is very hot. Add the bananas and sauté over medium heat until golden and tender, approximately 2 to 3 minutes on each side.

✱ To serve, scoop some frozen yogurt or ice cream, if desired, onto the center of each plate. Arrange the bananas around the yogurt and drizzle the caramel sauce around the entire plate. Garnish with the candied spiced almonds.

Crazy Berries

SERVES 6

This dessert, called *lampone pazzo* in Italian, was created by Michael Chiarello. You can use whatever berries are in season. You can use a store-bought mango- or raspberry-infused vinegar or make your own following the directions included here. Reprinted from *Flavored Vinegars* (Chronicle Books).

Vanilla-Scented Sugar Syrup

4 cups sugar

1 cup water

2 vanilla beans, minced, or 2 teaspoons
    pure vanilla extract

Mango Vinegar

2 large, ripe mangoes, peeled and
    cut into $1/2$-inch dice (approximately
    2 $1/2$ cups)

$1/2$ cup vanilla-scented sugar syrup
    (from above)

Pinch of salt

$1/2$ cup champagne vinegar

2 cups fresh berries, such as raspberries,
    strawberries, or blueberries

$1/2$ cup superfine sugar

6 tablespoons mango vinegar
    (from left)

Pinch of salt and freshly ground pepper

Sweetened whipped cream or
    mascarpone cheese, for garnish
    (optional)

✳ To make the vanilla-scented sugar syrup, put the sugar, water and vanilla beans, if using, in a pot and bring to a boil over high heat. Lower heat to a simmer and cook approximately 4 minutes. Stir occasionally. Let cool. Purée the syrup in a blender until vanilla beans are throughly chopped into the syrup. Strain through a fine strainer into a jar. If using vanilla extract instead of beans, add extract after the sugar syrup has cooled and pour into a jar. Seal tightly. Makes approximately 3 ¼ cups.

✳ To make your own mango vinegar, purée the mangoes, ½ cup of the sugar syrup, and salt together in a blender. Add the vinegar and taste to balance. Add more vinegar and thin with water if necessary. Strain through a fine strainer into a bowl or pitcher. Store in a clean jar or bottle (do not use metal lids or tops) and refrigerate. Makes approximately 2 ½ cups mango vinegar.

✳ In a nonreactive bowl, combine the berries, sugar, mango vinegar, salt and pepper and set aside to marinate for 5 to 10 minutes.

✳ To serve, place the berries in individual bowls and garnish with a dollop of whipped cream or mascarpone, if desired.

Caramelized Apple Tarts

Flaky Sweet Pastry

1 1/4 cups all-purpose flour

1/2 cup unsalted butter, chilled and
    cut into small pieces

1 tablespoon sugar

Pinch of salt

3 tablespoons ice water

4 tart apples such as Golden Delicious
    or Granny Smith

4 tablespoons unsalted butter

1/4 cup sugar

1 egg

Pinch of salt

1 tablespoon brown sugar (optional)

✳ To make the pastry, place the flour, butter, sugar, and salt in a food processor. Pulse 6 or 7 seconds, just until the mixture is the size of lima beans. With the machine running, add the ice water and pulse 3 or 4 times, just until the pastry begins to hold together. Do not let it form a ball.

✳ Remove the pastry from the machine. Place on a floured surface and shape into four small disks approximately 3 inches in diameter and 1/2-inch thick. Refrigerate for at least 1 hour or up to 2 days.

✳ Preheat the oven to 425° F.

✳ Peel and core the apples. Cut each into 12 even wedges.

✳ In a large skillet, melt the butter over medium-high heat. When it is hot but not quite smoking, add the apples, sprinkle with the sugar, and sauté until golden brown, approximately 10 minutes. Set aside to cool.

✳ Roll the dough into 7-inch circles, place the circles on an ungreased baking sheet, and set in the refrigerator for 10 minutes.

✳ In a small cup, whisk the egg with a pinch of salt.

✳ Place the apples in the center of each pastry circle in a circular pattern, leaving a 1-inch border around the edges. Fold the edges inward, making a fluted pattern. Brush the tops of the pastry with the beaten egg.

✳ Bake the tarts for approximately 20 minutes, or until golden on top. Sprinkle with brown sugar, if desired. Serve warm or at room temperature.

Baked Apples

SERVES 6

Few other desserts
fill the house with
such a wonderful
fragrance as they
cook than apples.
These can be baked
up to 8 hours before
serving. If you like,
serve them with
a dollop of cream,
crème fraîche,
sweetened yogurt,
or vanilla ice cream.
Reprinted from *Casual
Occasion Cookbook*
(Weldon Owen).

6 large Rome Beauty apples

Finely grated zest of 1 orange

6 tablespoons chopped raisins

1/4 cup firmly packed brown sugar

1/4 cup unsalted butter, at room temperature

1 teaspoon ground cinnamon

1/4 cup honey

1/2 cup fresh orange juice or apple cider

✳ Preheat the oven to 350° F.

✳ Core the apples to within 1/2 inch of the base, then peel them only halfway down from the top. Place side by side in a baking dish.

✳ In a small bowl, stir together the orange zest, raisins, brown sugar, butter, and cinnamon until well mixed. Divide this mixture evenly among the apples, pushing it down into the apple cavities.

✳ In a small saucepan over medium heat, combine the honey and orange juice or cider and heat just until the honey dissolves. Pour the honey mixture evenly over the apples and bake, basting often with the pan juices, until the apples are tender when pierced with a fork, approximately 45 minutes.

✳ To serve, let cool to room temperature. Place on individual plates and spoon the pan juices over the top.

Peachy Apple Cobbler

1 pound McIntosh or Winesap apples
1/2 cup dried peaches
4 eggs
3/4 cup sugar
2 teaspoons vanilla extract

1 tablespoon rum
1 cup all-purpose flour
1 1/2 cups milk, preferably low-fat
  or skim
Frozen vanilla yogurt and powdered
  sugar, for garnish (optional)

✽ Peel, quarter, and slice the apples into 1/8-inch-thick slices. Coarsely chop the peaches. Set aside.

✽ In an electric mixer, beat the eggs and sugar until fluffy. Add the vanilla and rum and beat again. Slowly add the flour until fully incorporated; then add the milk and beat until mixed well.

✽ Preheat the oven to 350° F. Lightly grease a 9- x 12-inch baking dish. Spread the apples and peaches evenly across the bottom of the dish. Pour the batter over the fruit.

✽ Bake for 40 to 45 minutes, or until the top of the cobbler is golden brown and a toothpick inserted in the center comes out clean. Serve warm with a scoop of frozen vanilla yogurt and powdered sugar, if desired.

SERVES 6

You can vary this cobbler by substituting other dried fruit for the peaches, such as dried apricots, blueberries, or cherries. If you are concerned about cholesterol, you can use 3 eggs and 2 egg whites in place of the 4 eggs.

Ginger Steamed Pudding

2 cups all-purpose flour

1 teaspoon baking soda

1/8 teaspoon salt

4 teaspoons ground ginger

3/4 cup unsalted butter, cut into cubes

1 cup firmly packed dark brown sugar

4 eggs

6 ounces crystallized ginger, coarsely
    chopped and lightly dusted with flour
    to prevent sticking

1 cup heavy cream

2 to 3 tablespoons confectioners' sugar

1 teaspoon grated orange zest

SERVES 6 TO 8

This holiday dessert is the perfect alternative to the traditional plum pudding. Reprinted from *Casual Occasions Cookbook* (Weldon Owen).

✳ Butter a deep, heatproof 1½-quart bowl, a metal steamed-pudding mold with a cover (preferably with a tube), or similar mold. Set aside. Place a wire trivet in a large, deep pot and fill approximately one-fourth full with water. Bring to a boil. Reduce the heat to low but keep hot. Bring a teakettle of water to a boil; keep warm.

✳ Sift together the flour, baking soda, salt, and ground ginger. Set aside.

✳ In a bowl, combine the butter and brown sugar and, if using an electric mixer, beat at medium speed until light and creamy, 3 to 4 minutes. Add the eggs, one at a time, beating well after each addition. Using a rubber spatula, fold in the flour mixture, one-third at a time, until blended. Stir in the chopped ginger.

✳ To avoid air pockets, carefully spoon the mixture into the prepared mold and then tap the mold on the countertop to level it off. The mold should be approximately two-thirds full, to allow for expansion. Attach the cover or fit a piece of parchment paper or aluminum foil greased with butter over the top (buttered-side down) and secure with kitchen string. Place the mold atop the trivet in the pot. The water should reach approximately halfway up the sides of the mold; add more boiling water as needed. Bring the water in the pot back to a low boil, reduce the heat, cover the pot and simmer for 2 hours if using a heatproof bowl, or 1½ hours if using a metal mold. To test for doneness, insert a toothpick into the center of the pudding; it should come out clean. Transfer from the pot to a rack. Uncover and let stand for 10 to 15 minutes.

✳ Meanwhile, in a bowl beat the cream, using a whisk, until it begins to thicken. Add the confectioners' sugar to taste and the orange zest. Continue whisking until soft peaks form that hold their shape. Do not beat until stiff.

✳ Invert the pudding onto a serving plate. Slice the warm pudding into wedges and transfer to plates. Top with the flavored whipped cream and serve with fresh berries, if desired.

Orange-Pistachio Torte with Ricotta and Fresh Fruit

SERVES 12

With its jeweled crown of fresh fruit, this cake, from Marlene Sorosky, is as pretty as a still life. Reprinted from *Entertaining on the Run* (William Morrow & Co.).

Orange-Pistachio Cake

1 medium orange

1/3 cup plus 1/3 cup sugar

2 cups shelled, unsalted pistachio nuts, chopped (approximately 10 1/2 ounces)

1/2 cup plus 1 tablespoon all-purpose flour

3/4 teaspoon baking powder

1/8 teaspoon salt

9 large eggs, separated

3/4 cup orange marmalade

1 1/2 teaspoons vanilla extract

Ricotta Filling

2 cups whole-milk or part-skim ricotta cheese (approximately 1 pound)

1/4 cup frozen orange juice concentrate, thawed

1/3 cup confectioners' sugar

Assorted fresh fruits, such as oranges, berries, sliced kiwi, sliced plums, sliced nectarines, red and green grapes, and sliced papaya

✷ To make the cake, preheat the oven to 350° F. Lightly grease two 8 1/2- or 9-inch layer-cake pans. Cut a circle of parchment or wax paper to fit the bottom and grease the paper.

✷ Using a sharp vegetable peeler, peel the orange zest, cutting off any white pith, which may be bitter. Reserve the fruit for the filling. Place the zest in a food processor with the metal blade. Add ⅓ cup sugar and process until finely ground, scraping the bottom and sides often. Add the nuts and pulse until finely ground. Pulse in the flour, baking powder, and salt.

✷ In a large mixing bowl, beat the egg yolks with ⅓ cup sugar until very thick and light, approximately 3 to 5 minutes. Mix in the marmalade and vanilla. On low speed, mix in the nut mixture just until incorporated.

✷ In a small mixing bowl with clean beaters, beat the egg whites until stiff-but-moist peaks form. Partially fold a third of the whites into the nut mixture and then fold in the remainder. Divide the batter between the prepared pans. Bake for 25 to 30 minutes, or until a toothpick inserted in the center comes out clean. Remove to racks and let cool for 20 minutes. Run a sharp knife around the sides and let cool for 30 minutes more. Invert onto racks to cool completely. (Cakes may be wrapped in foil and stored at room temperature overnight or frozen.)

✷ To make the filling, drain off any excess liquid from the ricotta. In a mixing bowl with an electric mixer, beat the ricotta until thick and light, approximately 2 minutes. Mix in the orange juice concentrate and confectioners' sugar.

✽ To assemble (up to 8 hours before serving), cut each cake layer in half horizontally. This is easiest to do on a turntable, marking the cake with toothpicks and using a serrated knife. Place one cake layer cut-side up on the cake plate. Spread with ½ cup filling. Top with the second cake layer cut-side up and spread with ½ cup filling. Halve the orange and slice it ¼-inch thick. Arrange a thick layer of orange and other fruit filling. Top with a third cake layer, spread with ½ cup filling, and top with the final cake layer, cut-side down. Spread the top with the remaining filling and arrange the fruit attractively on top. Cover with plastic wrap and refrigerate for at least 1 hour. The torte may be refrigerated up to 8 hours.

Strawberries in a Sea of Mango

1 large mango, peeled and pitted
2 tablespoons fresh lime juice
1 tablespoon sugar

1 pint strawberries, hulled and quartered
Fresh mint leaves, for garnish

✽ Place the mango, 1 tablespoon lime juice, and 1 teaspoon sugar in a food processor fitted with the metal blade or in a blender and purée. You should have approximately 1 cup of purée.

✽ In a nonreactive bowl, toss the strawberries with the remaining lime juice and sugar and let sit for 15 to 30 minutes if possible to draw out their juices.

✽ To serve, spoon ¼ cup mango puree onto a dessert plate or bowl and top with strawberries. Garnish with mint and serve.

SERVES 4

This sensuous, beautiful dessert, from Martha Rose Schulman, always gets raves at her dinner parties. The mango purée can be made a day ahead of time and stored in the refrigerator. The strawberries can be prepared a few hours before serving. Reprinted from *Mexican Light* (Bantam Books).

S'more Pie

Crust
1 1/2 cups graham cracker crumbs
6 tablespoons unsalted butter, melted

Filling
1 1/2 cups whipping cream
12 ounces semisweet or milk chocolate,
    finely chopped
2 teaspoons pure vanilla extract
2 (7-ounce) jars marshmallow creme

✳ To prepare the crust, preheat the oven to 350° F and butter a 9-inch pie pan. In a medium bowl, combine the graham cracker crumbs and the melted butter and turn them into the pie pan. Use the back of a large spoon to press the mixture firmly and evenly over the bottom and up the sides of the pan. Bake for 10 minutes. Cool completely before filling.

✳ To prepare the filling, in a 4-cup glass measuring cup, combine the cream and chocolate. Microwave on High for 1 1/2 minutes; stir well. Microwave 1 more minute; stir until the mixture is smooth and creamy. (The mixture may require an additional 30 seconds of heating, depending on the microwave wattage.) Alternatively, combine the cream and chocolate in a medium saucepan. Heat over medium-low heat, stirring often, until the chocolate is melted and the mixture is smooth. For either method, stir the vanilla into the melted chocolate mixture, blending well. Pour into the cooled crust and refrigerate for at least 4 hours.

✳ Position the rack 4 inches from the broiling unit and preheat the broiler. Spoon dollops of marshmallow creme over the surface of the pie. Gently spread over the surface leaving a 1-inch border around the edges of the crust (the marshmallow will spread when heated). If you're using a glass pie plate, place the pie in the middle of a 10- x 15-inch jelly-roll pan; surround the plate with ice cubes. (This will prevent the broiler heat from cracking the cold pie plate; it's not necessary to do this with a metal pan.) Broil the pie until the marshmallow surface is browned to your liking, turning the pan as necessary for even heat.

✳ Serve immediately or refrigerate until ready to serve. Use a serrated blade to decrease the possibility of the top's cracking when you cut through the thin layer of crisp toasted marshmallow.

SERVES 8 TO 10

This delicious and easy pie will bring back childhood memories of campfire s'mores. Sharon Tyler Herbst created this pie at the request of her 12-year-old nephew. You can shortcut this recipe by using a store-bought crust. Serve with fresh berries, if desired. Reprinted from *The Food Lover's Guide to Chocolate and Vanilla* (William Morrow & Co.).

Bête Noire with White Chocolate Cream

SERVES 8 TO 12

Lora Brody's delicious and unusual chocolate dessert is a snap to make—either by hand or in a food processor. Eaten hot out of the oven, it's a perfect marriage between a soufflé and a truffle. Served at room temperature with white chocolate cream, it ranks right up there with the world's best chocolate experience. Reprinted from *Growing Up on the Chocolate Diet* (Little, Brown & Co.).

White Chocolate Cream (*must be made at least a day in advance*)

12 ounces best quality white chocolate, cut into small pieces

1/2 cup heavy cream

2/3 cup white chocolate liqueur

Bête Noire

8 ounces unsweetened chocolate

4 ounces bittersweet chocolate

1 1/3 cups superfine sugar

1/2 cup water

1 cup unsalted butter, at room temperature, cut into 10 chunks

5 extra-large eggs, at room temperature

✱ To make the white chocolate cream, place the pieces of white chocolate in the work bowl of a food processor or blender. Combine the cream and the white chocolate liqueur in a small saucepan. Heat to just below boiling and then pour over the chocolate and blend or process until completely smooth. You may add up to 1/3 cup additional liqueur if desired. Chill completely. The cream will keep for 1 week in the refrigerator.

✱ To make the Bête Noire, preheat the oven to 350° F with the rack in the center position. Lightly grease a 9-inch layer-cake pan and then line the bottom with a 9-inch circle of parchment. Lightly grease the parchment. Set the cake pan in a jelly-roll pan or roasting pan.

✱ Chop both the chocolates into fine pieces and set them aside.

✱ **To prepare the cake by hand:** Combine 1 cup of the sugar and the water in a medium-sized saucepan, and stirring occasionally, cook over medium heat until the sugar dissolves and the mixture comes to a vigorous boil. Turn off the heat and immediately add the chocolate pieces to the boiling syrup and stir until they are completely dissolved. Stir in the butter, one chunk at a time, stirring until each chunk is incorporated before adding the next. Beat the eggs together with the remaining 1/3 cup of sugar until they are foamy and slightly thickened and then whisk them into the chocolate, beating well to incorporate all the ingredients. Pour and scrape the mixture into the prepared pan and level the batter with a rubber scraper.

✱ **To prepare the cake in a food processor:** Place the chocolate in the work bowl of a food processor. Crack the eggs into a spouted cup. Combine the 1 ⅓ cups sugar and the water in a saucepan and, stirring occasionally, cook over medium heat until the sugar dissolves and the mixture comes to a vigorous boil. Pour the boiling syrup over chocolate, cover the processor with the feed tube in place, and process for 12 seconds, or until the chocolate is completely melted and the mixture is smooth. With the machine on, add the butter one chunk at a time, then add the eggs. Process for an additional 15 seconds. Pour and scrape the batter into the prepared pan, leveling the top with a rubber scraper.

✱ To bake, place the cake pan and jelly-roll pan (or roasting pan) in the oven and pour hot water to the depth of 1 inch into the larger pan. Bake for exactly 30 minutes. The top will have a thin dry crust, but the inside will be very moist. Carefully remove the cake pan from the oven (leave the water bath until it cools.)

✱ Cover the top of the cake with a piece of plastic wrap. Invert the cake onto a flat plate or baking sheet. Peel off the parchment. Cover with a light, flat plate and immediately invert again.

✱ Serve hot or at room temperature with a dollop of the white chocolate cream.

Banana Layer Cake with Peanut Butter Buttercream

SERVES 8 TO 12

Wayne Brachman created this layer cake to emulate the dramatic stratified rock formations found in the Southwest. This layer cake has strata of banana cake and peanut butter frosting that run vertically instead of horizontally. Plan on starting this cake a day ahead; the cake layers need to set in the freezer for at least 4 hours. Reprinted from *Cakes and Cowpokes* (William Morrow & Co.).

Banana Cake

2 1/2 cups cake flour

1 teaspoon baking soda

1/4 teaspoon baking powder

1/4 teaspoon salt

12 tablespoons unsalted butter,
    at room temperature

1 1/4 cups sugar

3 large eggs, at room temperature

3 large very ripe bananas

1/2 cup sour cream

1 tablespoon vanilla extract

Peanut Butter Buttercream

16 tablespoons (1/2 cup) unsalted butter,
    at room temperature

1 (18-ounce) jar creamy peanut butter

2 1/2 cups confectioners' sugar

Decorations

1/2 cup whole unsalted peanuts, plus
    1/2 cup chopped unsalted peanuts

1 ounce semisweet chocolate, melted

✱ To make the cake, set a rack in the middle of the oven and preheat to 375° F. Lightly grease the sides of two 15½- x 10-inch jelly-roll pans. Line them with parchment or buttered wax paper.

✱ Sift the flour, baking soda, baking powder, and salt together onto a sheet of waxed paper. Sift two more times to mix and aerate.

✱ Put the butter and sugar in the bowl of an electric mixer and beat at high speed for 30 seconds, or until well combined and smooth. Add the eggs one at a time, beating until each is incorporated. Continue beating, scraping down the sides of the bowl if necessary, until the mixture is light and fluffy and doubled in volume, approximately 5 more minutes.

✱ In a small bowl, using the mixer or a fork, mash the bananas until soupy. Stir in the sour cream and vanilla.

✱ With the mixer on its lowest setting, or using a rubber spatula, beat or fold one-third of the flour mixture into the butter mixture. Beat or fold in half of the banana mixture, then another third of the flour mixture. Beat or fold in the remaining banana mixture and then the remaining flour mixture.

✱ Divide the batter between the prepared pans, spreading it evenly with an offset metal spatula. Bake for 15 minutes, or until just golden and the centers spring back when lightly pressed. Cool the cakes in the pan on wire racks.

✴ To make the buttercream, put the butter and peanut butter in the bowl of an electric mixer and beat at medium speed until blended. Reduce the speed to low and gradually beat in the sugar. Increase the speed to medium and beat for 3 minutes, or until smooth and fluffy.

✴ To assemble the cake, cover each cake with a sheet of waxed paper or parchment paper. Place a large baking sheet over one cake, and carefully flip the cake over. Peel off the parchment. With a serrated knife or a pizza wheel, trim the edges of the cake. Using a ruler as a guide, cut ten 2- x 15-inch strips from the cake. Repeat with the second cake. Reserve one-third of the buttercream, and spread the remaining buttercream evenly over the cake strips.

✴ Disassemble a 9-inch springform pan, and wrap the bottom in plastic wrap. Tightly roll one cake strip up like a jelly roll, and stand it on end in the center of the pan bottom. Coil the remaining strips around the first, butting the ends together to form one large spiral. Fit the side pieces of the springform on and snap it closed. Freeze for at least 4 hours, or overnight.

✴ Just before serving, make the decorations. Arrange the whole peanuts in little clusters on a plate covered with waxed paper. Melt the chocolate in a small bowl set over a saucepan of barely simmering water. Using a fork, drizzle the chocolate over the peanuts. Refrigerate for 15 minutes to set.

✴ Soak a towel in hot water and squeeze dry. Wrap it around the springform pan to loosen the sides. Remove the sides of the pan and invert the cake onto a serving platter or cardboard cake round. Using a metal spatula, frost the top and sides of the cake with the reserved buttercream. Press the chopped peanuts into the sides of the cake, and decorate the top with the chocolate-covered peanut clusters. Serve at room temperature. The cake can be covered and stored in the refrigerator for up to 3 days.

Tunnel of Fudge Cheesecake

Cookies 'n' Cream Crust

1 1/2 cups Oreo or Hydrox cookie crumbs (approximately 22 cookies), including the filling

3 tablespoons unsalted butter, melted

5 (8-ounce) packages cream cheese, softened

1 1/2 cups sugar

5 eggs

1/4 cup all-purpose flour

1/2 teaspoon salt

1/4 cup whipping cream

3 ounces semisweet chocolate, melted and cooled

1/2 cup semisweet chocolate chips

1 tablespoon pure vanilla extract

Sweetened whipped cream

✴ To make the Cookies 'n' Cream Crust, preheat the oven to 350° F. Lightly grease a 9-inch springform pie pan. In a medium bowl, stir together the cookie crumbs and butter. Turn mixture into the prepared pan with the back of a large spoon, pressing firmly and evenly over the bottom and up the sides of the pan. Bake for 10 minutes; let cool to room temperature. Raise the heat to 400° F.

✴ In a large bowl, beat the cream cheese and sugar together until smooth and fluffy. Add the eggs, one at a time, beating after each addition. Beat in the flour, salt, and cream.

✴ Place 2 cups of the cheese mixture in a medium bowl. Stirring constantly, gradually add the melted chocolate, blending until well combined. Stir in the chocolate chips; set aside. Stir the vanilla into the remaining cheese mixture.

✴ Pour all but 1½ cups light cheese mixture into the prepared crust. Spoon the chocolate-cheese filling in a 2-inch-wide ring onto the light cheese mixture, 1½ inches from the edge of the pan. Do not get any in the center of the light mixture. Using the back of a spoon, press the chocolate mixture down into the light mixture until the top is level. Spoon the reserved light cheese mixture evenly over all and smooth the top.

✴ Place the cheesecake in the center of the middle oven rack. Position a 13- x 9-inch baking pan filled halfway with hot water on a lower shelf. Bake for 15 minutes. Reduce the heat to 300° F; bake an additional 50 minutes.

✴ Turn the oven off. Let the cheesecake cool in the oven for 1 hour with the oven door open 1 to 3 inches. Remove cheesecake from the oven to a rack; let cool completely. Cover and refrigerate overnight.

✴ To serve, run a thin knife around the inside edge of the pan; remove the side of the pan. Use a thin knife to loosen the crust from the bottom of the pan. With two large metal spatulas, carefully slide the cheesecake off the pan bottom and onto a serving plate. Spread the whipped cream over the top. Chill for at least 1 hour before serving.

SERVES 10 TO 12

It was Mae West who said "Too much of a good thing can be wonderful" and Sharon Tyler Herbst who not only dug up the quotation but also created this show-stopper dessert, which gets top votes from her students. This cheesecake needs to be made a day before serving. Avoid using double-stuffed Oreo cookies for the crust. Reprinted from *The Food Lover's Guide to Chocolate and Vanilla* (William Morrow & Co.).

RECIPE INDEX BY TELEVISION EPISODE

INDEX

The **KitchenAid**® Story

A HUMBLE BEGINNING *The modern KitchenAid stand mixer began with a single drop of sweat off the end of a busy baker's nose. The year was 1908, and Herbert Johnston, an engineer and later president of the Hobart Manufacturing Company in Troy, Ohio, was watching the baker mix bread dough with an age-old iron spoon. To help ease that burden, Johnston pioneered the development of an eighty-quart mixer. By 1915 professional bakers had an easier, more thorough, and more sanitary way of mixing their wares.*

In fact, that amazing, labor-saving machine caught on so quickly that the United States Navy ordered Hobart mixers for its three new battleships—The California, The Tennessee, and The South Carolina. By 1917 the mixer was classified as "regular equipment" on all U.S. Navy ships.

The success of the commercial mixer gave Hobart engineers inspiration to create a mixer suitable for the home. But World War I interfered, and the concept of a home mixer was put on hold.

1919

THE BIRTH OF A KITCHEN ICON

1919 was truly a time of change. The gray days of war were giving way to the gaiety of the Roaring Twenties. The spark of women's suffrage had ignited and women across America would soon earn the right to vote. America was on the brink of an era of peace and prosperity, and progress was the cry from the factory to the farm.

War munitions plants across the country were busily converting to peace-time production. Meanwhile, a small manufacturing company in a sleepy, southwest Ohio town revived its effort to design the first electrical "food preparer" for the home.

And so it did! The first home stand mixer was born in 1919 at the Troy Metal Products Company, a subsidiary of the Hobart Manufacturing Company. The progeny of the large commercial food mixers, the Model H-5 was the first in a long line of quality home food preparers that utilized "planetary action." Planetary action was a revolutionary design that rotated the beater in one direction while moving it around the bowl in the opposite direction.

The wives of Troy executives tested the initial prototypes. While discussing possible names for the new machine, one homemaker commented, "I don't care what you call it, but I know it's the best kitchen aid I have ever had!" Hence, a brand name was born, and the first KitchenAid stand mixer was unveiled to the American consumer.

> "I don't care what you call it, but I know it's the best kitchen aid I have ever had!"

The KitchenAid H-5 rolled off the newly founded KitchenAid Manufacturing Company's assembly line at the rate of four per day and was priced at $189.50. The overriding concern then, as now, was that every KitchenAid produced would be of unsurpassed quality. Nothing would be shipped to customers that was not tested and retested.

But retail dealers were reluctant to undertake the selling of the unique "food preparer." So KitchenAid set out to sell its stand mixers door-to-door with a largely female sales force (strong enough to carry the 65-lb. Model H-5 on sales calls). Homemakers were encouraged to invite friends to their homes, where the KitchenAid salesperson would prepare food for the group showcasing the new stand mixer. By the 1930s the KitchenAid had earned wide acceptance, and dealers began to show interest.

1920–1930s

MEETING THE CONSUMERS' NEEDS

In the mid-1920s production had increased to five mixers per day, which was considered excellent efficiency by the standards of the day. Prices had declined to $150 (approximately $1,500 in today's dollars), and the company offered an easy payment program of 10% down and 10% per month for 10 months with no interest.

By the late 1920s American kitchens were growing smaller. KitchenAid responded with a smaller, lighter stand mixer at a lower price. The Model G proved so popular that the Model H-5 was stopped.

1930s

The 1930s brought the Depression, and with it, rising unemployment. The model G was beyond the financial means of most Americans, so KitchenAid confronted the problem. Within three years Kitchen-Aid introduced three new models that were less expensive and within the means of many American households.

In the midst of the great dust bowl years, social upheaval, and joblessness, KitchenAid planners laid a solid foundation that would support the stand mixer's growth for the next six decades. KitchenAid recruited Egmont Arens, a nationally acclaimed editor and world-renowned designer, to design three new stand mixer models. Arens's designs were so timelessly simple and functional that they remain virtually unchanged to this day.

1937

THE MODEL K

The Model K, first introduced in 1937, was more compact, moderately priced ($55), and capable of powering all the attachments. Every model introduced since has allowed for fully interchangeable attachments—a tribute to common sense and management of resources.

By the late 1930s, demand for KitchenAid stand mixers was so great that the factory could not keep up and sold out before Christmas each year. But in 1941 World War II intervened and the plant focused its production on munitions. During the war years there was limited production of KitchenAid stand mixers.

> ...the name KitchenAid has become synonymous with quality to generations of Americans.

As peace arrived and the troops came home, production of the KitchenAid stand mixer began again in earnest. KitchenAid moved to Greenville, Ohio, to expand the production. Greenville, is still the home of the factory where the dedicated employees of that community have proudly produced the stand mixer, and now other KitchenAid products, for more than half a century.

1950–1997

SEEN IN ALL THE BEST PLACES

KitchenAid, always in the forefront of trends, introduced daring new colors at the 1955 Atlantic City Housewares Show. The new colors—Petal Pink, Sunny Yellow, Island Green, Satin Chrome, and Antique Copper—were a bold departure from the white appliances seen in most kitchens of the time. To this day KitchenAid offers the standard classics, along with a variety of decorative colors.

Today, the legacy of quality lives on not only in the multifunctional stand mixer, but also in a full line of kitchen appliances sold across the world. Every product that carries the KitchenAid name, whether purchased in Paris or Peoria, is guaranteed to be strong, reliable and versatile—each backed by over 75 years of quality and excellence.

The distinctive silhouette of KitchenAid appliances can be seen in some of America's most famous home and restaurant kitchens. "Home Cooking" with Amy Coleman—which KitchenAid is proud to sponsor as part of an ongoing commitment to nurturing the talents of home chefs—marks the latest of many cooking shows that have relied on KitchenAid appliances to perform faultlessly and enhance the decor of their sets. Viewers of "Friends," "Cybill," and other television shows will see the appliances prominently displayed, and even used on occasion, in these sitcom kitchens. And finding a top restaurant without at least one hard-working KitchenAid stand mixer would be a real challenge.

Even museums, the ultimate showcases for design excellence, feature KitchenAid products on display. San Francisco's avant-garde Museum of Modern Art, for example, featured the KitchenAid stand mixer in an exhibit of American icons. There is even a KitchenAid stand mixer in the esteemed collection of the Smithsonian Institution.

From humble beginnings among the cornfields of southwest Ohio, the name KitchenAid has become synonymous with quality. Although over the years KitchenAid has streamlined and updated its stand mixer design and technology, the worldwide success of KitchenAid can be traced to the solid foundation set back in 1919.